Encouraging Words...

Also by Dennis Merritt Jones

How to Speak Science of Mind
(DeVorss Publishing)

The Art of Being:
101 Ways to Practice Purpose in Your Life
(Tarcher / Penguin / Random House)

The Art of Uncertainty:
How to Live in the Mystery of Life
and Love It
(Tarcher / Penguin / Random House)

Your (Re)Defining Moments:
Becoming Who You Were Born to Be
(Tarcher / Penguin / Random House)

TO BE RELEASED IN 2018:

The Art of Abundance:
Ten Rules for a Prosperous Life
(Tarcher / Perigree / Penguin Random House)

More Praise for *Encouraging Words*

In his book Encouraging Words, *Dennis Merritt Jones creates a woven fabric of storytelling which wakes up what is lying dormant within us—the depth of our hearts we are all longing to reach.*

TEMPLE HAYES
Spiritual Leader, Author, Difference Maker

Encouraging Words *is more than just a life-preserver of hope for a drowning world. It is a book of wisdom and guidance, written by one of the world's most heartfelt spiritual leaders, Dr. Dennis Merritt Jones. Keep this book at your bedside. Read an excerpt each morning or night. It will uplift and inspire you to greatness.*

DR. CHRIS MICHAELS
Author of *The Power of You: How to Live Your Authentic, Exciting, Joy-Filled Life Now*

In Encouraging Words, *Dennis Merritt Jones brings wisdom, clarity, and possibility into the lives of anyone who cares to read this thoughtful collection. He shows that even a modest shift in perspective can change one's life for the better.*

JIM LOCKARD
Author of Creating the Beloved Community

In this inspiring collection, Dennis reminds us that there lies within each of us an explorer who yearns for higher ground. One might think of these essays as a road map that doesn't merely promise a glorious destination, but actually leads us there one page at a time. That the terrain is alternately ragged and serene only fortifies the realistic value of the journey which (spoiler alert!) ultimately leads where it begins—within the sacred heart of each of us.

DR. BARBARA E. FIELDS
Executive Director, Association for Global New Thought

Encouraging Words...

ARTICLES & ESSAYS THAT PROVE Who You Are Matters

DENNIS MERRITT JONES

Award-Winning Author
and *Science of Mind* Magazine Columnist

foreword by
David S. Goldberg, Ph.D.

573 Park Point Drive
Golden, Colorado 80401-7042

www.DennisMerrittJones.com

Spiritual Living Press
573 Park Point Drive
Golden, Colorado 80401-7402

Printed in the United States of America
Published September 2017

COVER DESIGN & BOOK LAYOUT MARIA ROBINSON, DESIGNS ON YOU, LLC
LITTLETON, COLORADO 80121

ISBN e-book: 978-0-917849-63-3
ISBN: 978-0-917849-62-6

THIS BOOK IS DEDICATED **TO MY TEACHERS**

Dr. Ernest **Holmes**

Dr. William **Hornaday**

Dr. Raymond Charles **Barker**

Dr. Carleton **Whitehead**

Dr. Fletcher **Harding**

Dr. Frank **Richelieu**

Rev. William T. **Curtiss**

It has been said that we stand on the shoulders of giants.
These giants pointed the way; they proved to me
that who I am—and what I do with who I am—matters.
As you read this book may you realize
the same is true about you.

YOU MATTER.

Table of **Contents**

Foreword

One of the great joys of my work as a publisher is to work with extraordinary people to help bring their light to the world. Dennis Merritt Jones is one of those unique voices. As a reader of *Science of Mind* magazine, I was familiar with Dennis's work long before I became the publisher of the publication. Once I stepped into the role of publisher, it soon became apparent that Dennis was one of our readers' favorite writers.

As we have continued to work together over the years, Dennis approached me with the idea of creating a compilation of some of his essays for the magazine, along with some new work. It was a conversation that I welcomed, and we soon agreed that the same organization that publishes *Science of Mind* magazine would also be a good fit to publish this, his latest book.

Science of Mind magazine is one of the largest, digest-sized magazines in the country. We honor all people and all paths to the Divine. Our philosophy is Oneness and it is our honor to support people on their unique spiritual paths. This year we are celebrating ninety years of continuous publication. We touch 80,000 people on a monthly basis with the magazine in all of its forms. Additionally, we have almost 500,000 Facebook friends in our online community and we reach another 30,000 people with our free bimonthly newsletter. Please visit www.scienceofmind.com to sign up and to learn more about us.

Dennis and I had an opportunity to meet face-to-face last year when I was in Florida. Our conversation was fluid and covered a lot of ground, from his ongoing work with the magazine to recent personal losses, and from his beloved four-legged Mac to his relocation from California to Florida.

I was excited to receive the draft of *Encouraging Words* and wasn't disappointed. The book captures the best of Dennis's articles with the same depth and breadth of Dennis himself. You'll find conversations that incorporate philosophy, religion, psychology, spirituality, New Thought and music. One of the many things I appreciate about this work is that you can read it from cover-to-cover or you can open it up and let the Universe guide you to what you need in the moment. I love that there are multiple points of entry.

Along with the personal and historical stories, Dennis offers practices to put what you've just read into direct application in your life—applied spirituality. It's what he's known for and so good at!

So whether through his words, a song, a quote, or a mindfulness practice, I invite you to settle in and enjoy this yummy compilation of some of the best work of Dennis Merritt Jones. To paraphrase a line from the play *Auntie Mame,* enjoy this delectable treat from the "buffet of life!"

With Great Love,
David

Rev. Dr. David Goldberg
Golden, CO
June 28, 2017

Introduction

As a writer, I know that words are important at the beginning of any creative process; they become the tools used to convey ideas—to paint a picture that holds relevance and meaning to the reader and hopefully finds a home in their heart. Between the covers of this book are many words which are intended to offer you encouragement, irrespective of who you are or where you are on this sometimes challenging, sometimes confusing, sometimes exhilarating journey we call life.

My personal vision is "Guiding People to Purpose." It is my belief that we each have a purpose for being on this planet or we would not be here; we all matter. In this book you will find a compilation of articles I have been privileged to write for *Science of Mind* magazine, as well as a number of essays I have written as blogs over the years. As you read these articles and essays, may you be open to receiving the love and respect intended in each one. The content of this book is innately spiritual, and meant to be so, because that is what you are—a spiritual being having a human experience. When it is time for you to return to the place of your spiritual origin you will be asked two questions: Did you learn to love well . . . and, is the planet a better place today than it was the day you arrived because *you* were there? As you read this book, may the answer to these questions become a litmus test for the balance of your life that encourages you to live an exquisite, fulfilling life. Know that who you are and—equally important—what you *do* with who you are, matter.

PEACE,

DR. DENNIS MERRITT JONES

www.DennisMerrittJones.com

To contemplate something as etheric and yet as palpable as what we refer to as the heart of humanity is rather mind-boggling, and it beckons the questions: What exactly is the "heart of humanity" and where is it?

There Is Only One of Us Here

As we recognize our Oneness with Infinite Intelligence, we are set free from uncertainty and pain. As long as we realize that our heart is a living center, through which the Love of God flows to bless eternally, not only our own lives, but the lives of all whom we contact—as long as we realize this, our heart cannot be troubled.

~ ERNEST HOLMES, *THE SCIENCE OF MIND*

Often when the subject of "the heart" comes up, I flash back to 1992 when my dad was guided to go to the hospital because of chest pains, and within thirty minutes was under the knife receiving a quadruple bypass for an extreme heart condition known as "the widow maker." He went on to live another twenty-nine years in great health, ultimately passing at ninety-five years of age. While Dad had always been a spiritually grounded person, having his chest cracked open and his heart exposed to the "Light" deepened his sense of Oneness with Life. As a student of Science of Mind teaching for thirty-five years, he told me once there was never a doubt in his mind that while the doctors were mending his heart God was doing the healing and that the two worked together as One. Let us be clear: in this context, to "mend" is to set a broken bone, remove or repair a diseased organ, or stitch skin together. "Healing" occurs when the Infinite Life Force within is realized and revealed, and it is *always* an inside job. Simply put, "healing is the revealing" of God's presence at the center and circumference of an apparent condition. My dad knew that it was Divine Intelligence working in, through, and *as* the minds and hands of the doctors (as well as his own body) that did both the mending *and* the healing of his heart.

But, this is not just a story about my dad's heart. This is also about another heart that is in great need of mending and healing—the heart of humanity. When Ernest Holmes stated that the heart is a living center through which the Love of God flows to bless eternally, he was speaking of our human heart *and* the heart we all share—the heart of humanity. In either case, it is the vital pulsebeat of Infinite Intelligence operating at Its highest vibration—Love—that keeps the Life Force flowing. When that Life Force is blocked it is never good news for the patient . . . in this case, the patient being humankind. To contemplate something as etheric and yet as palpable as what we refer to as the heart of humanity is rather mind-boggling and it beckons the questions: What exactly is the "heart of humanity" and where is it? Once we find it and awaken to its need to be mended, how do we facilitate such a massive healing?

These are exacting questions because they invite us to become conscious participants in removing the blockages that stand between us and our collective well-being as a species. Many of us are aware that the heart of humanity needs our attention; we just don't know what to do about it. The good news is, metaphorically speaking, there are plenty of surgeons on standby to do the mending, and if you are reading this book you are most likely one of them.

To find the heart of humanity we need look
no further than our own deepest
knowing that affirms there is only One of us here.

The heart of humanity is a universal heartthrob—it pulsates at the center of every human being—it is that place within each of us where God has personalized Itself as unconditional Love. It knows it is one with something infinitely larger than what we see gazing back at us in the mirror. From a spiritual perspective that "something" is the One Infinite Intelligence that permeates the essence of all that is. From a secular perspective, the heart of humanity is the connective tissue that binds us to one another as sentient beings who are conscious that we all share a common home called planet Earth, and that what affects one of us surely must affect all of us.

Not Christian or Jew or Muslim, not Hindu,
Buddhist, Sufi, or Zen. Not any religion
or cultural system. I am not from the east
or the west, not out of the ocean or up from

> the ground, not natural or ethereal, not composed of elements at all . . . I belong to the beloved, have seen the two worlds as one and that one call to and know, first, last, outer, inner, only that breath breathing human being.
>
> ~ RUMI

The challenge, it seems, lies in mindfully applying the wisdom of Rumi when there is so much going on in our personal lives and in the world that appears to contradict our Oneness with each other. As we enter the relative world every day we are confronted with a collective consciousness that exists horizontally on the surface of life where duality reigns supreme, manifesting as judgment, hate, fear, anger, frustration, envy, resentment, prejudice, superiority, inferiority, and so on. The "inhumanity" that humanity is rendering to itself goes beyond any words to describe it; it truly is heartbreaking. We need look no further than our own communities and the world media to witness the heartbreak. The irony is that only humanity can mend its own heart. This is where we come in: by mindfully taking the vertical plunge to go within, below the surface of our horizontal life, and connecting with the sacred heart of the true Self that knows It is one with Life, we can consciously bring an awareness of Its presence to the surface where we integrate It with everything we say, think, and do. This is where our sacred "Being" merges with our human "doing" and it is how we each can do our part to help mend the heart of humanity. The practice is to remember that even though we do the mending, it is an awareness of God's presence in the moment that does the healing: we remove the blockage of our beliefs that impede the flow, separating us from one another, by remembering we are each the sacred arteries though which God's Love flows indiscriminately.

Reviving the Heart of Humanity with a New Kind of CPR

Mending the heart of humanity sounds like a daunting task, but if we are willing to be proactive and act mindfully, rather than react mindlessly (or hopelessly), it can be revived. We must each become experts at administering spiritual "CPR" (**C**ompassion, **P**atience and **R**everence) to every person with whom we cross paths on a daily basis. This includes our face-to-face encounters—both intentional and by chance—as well as the countless people we may connect with via the Internet or see on TV while watching the world news. Distance does not matter; because we all share the same name—Human Being—we all share the same heart.

COMPASSION

> If we are conscious we know there is something within us that is called to respond to the pain, fear, and suffering of others, be they our next door neighbors or strangers on the other side of the planet. How could we ignore them when we know we are all living branches, intertwined with one another on the Great Vine of Life? Compassion is the capacity to imagine what it must feel

like to live in another person's skin and take appropriate action to help alleviate suffering when possible. As Desmond Tutu put it, "My humanity is bound up in yours, for we can only be human together." When we embody true compassion, the differences between us disappear and reveal that which we have in common—a bridge that supersedes language, religion, politics, and cultural barriers, because it connects hearts with hearts.

PATIENCE

Healing the heart of humanity is the outcome of each of us realizing and revealing the presence of God in the present moment. Mending the heart of humanity is the process that gets us there, and it is one that may require time because it is our consciousness we are mending—we are reshaping it to hold a larger idea. Patience is the ability to breathe and be with what is in the moment, trusting that as we continue to mindfully mend our own hearts, one day at a time, the collective heart of humanity is also mending. The practice is to be patient with ourselves and all others, remembering it can take time to mend a broken heart—especially one that belongs to seven billion human beings.

REVERENCE

If we are willing to look deeply into one another, getting past all of our perceived differences, we will be able to see what we have in common; we'll remember there is really only One of us here. To practice reverence is to look past the form and see the sacred presence of God therein. Contained within the wisdom of this awareness lies the potential for the healing of the heart of humanity. How could we possibly conspire to do harm to another when we see ourselves and the living presence of the Divine in them?

After my dad's surgery, his life became a daily mindfulness practice of paying attention to what went into his body *and his mind;* he took the personal actions necessary to mend, heal, and, quite literally, keep his heart open. Our call as a species is to now do the same. Don't think for a minute that who *you* are and what you do with who you are doesn't matter. We are each stewards of the heart of humanity. Perhaps Dr. Holmes gave us the clearest message about how best to do our part in an affirmation he wrote in *The Science of Mind:*

> God in me is unified with God in all . . . I am
> one with all people, with all things, with all life.
> As I listen in the silence, the voice of all
> humanity speaks to me and answers the love
> that I hold out to it . . . I AM ONE WITH LIFE.
> I wait in the silence while the Great Spirit bears
> this message to the whole world.

As a mindfulness practice, consider printing this affirmation on multiple pieces of paper and posting them throughout your home. Then each time you see it, pause, take a deep breath ...listen in silence to the beat of your heart and know there are seven billion other hearts pulsating with the same Life Force at that very moment...and then smile, knowing you have just touched the heart of humanity.

THERE REALLY IS ONLY ONE OF US HERE.

If someone is "pushing your buttons" you might want to take a moment and explore how they got installed in the first place.

Who Is Chafing **Your Chaps?**

> Projection always hides a feeling you don't want to look at. If you examine any negative trait you insist is present in another person, you will find that same trait hiding in yourself. The more you deny this trait, the more strongly you will have to project it.
>
> ~ DR. DEEPAK CHOPRA

Recently in a radio interview a call-in listener asked me how to deal with certain irritating, objectionable people at the workplace. I responded by saying one doesn't even have to go as far as the workplace to find objectionable people—they are all around! We'll find them at the grocery store, on the freeway, on the street corner, over the backyard fence, on the television, and even in our own family—and they are there for a reason. It is the Universe offering us an endless supply of people necessary to help us see some aspect of our own character we may not necessarily see or like. Now, let us be clear, I am not talking about terrorists, despots, embezzlers, career criminals, or people who do horrendous and unspeakable things to others. I am referring to those common, garden variety, everyday folks we all know who just "rub us" the wrong way; such as someone who constantly complains, talks incessantly, gossips, tells white lies, is selfish, controlling, passive, opinionated, a braggart, abrasive, unkempt, perfectionistic, unreliable, perpetually late, irresponsible, or ___________ (fill in the blank). In other words, who is chafing your chaps? Having one's "chaps be chafed" is an old cowboy term for an irritation caused by too much friction between one's derrière and the saddle. While this is a colorful metaphor it clearly describes how we allow certain people we perceive to be a pain in the butt to get under our skin. The question is why? The irony is—if Chopra is right—we can run but we can't hide from ourselves. By means of the law of attraction these people will continue to show up in our lives until we learn the lesson. The sad part is many people will go to their grave having never learned the lesson because they are not willing to be honest with themselves by exploring their own inner emotional landscape. It takes courage and compassion to be willing to see a reflection of ourselves in those we don't like and mindfully respond rather than react to them. I am reminded of what one of my early spiritual mentors would say whenever I became chafed and overreacted to what he was saying: "While I may push your buttons, I didn't install them—you did." The good news is, with mindfulness, one can skillfully uninstall those buttons. But the first step is to become aware they are there.

How will we know when we are projecting?

The practice is to be present enough in the moment to witness the emotional response that bolts through our physical body when that certain person says or does something that pushes our buttons. What I have noticed personally is that when I come across such an individual, my first reaction is to want to withdraw—if not physically, emotionally. With mindfulness the awareness that arises in that moment is that this individual may be offering me a gift by serving as my mirror. It helps to remember that the more a person chafes us, the deeper the trigger point (trait) lies within ourselves. If this were not so, that person's presence and actions would have no effect on us. There must be some point within us that resonates with that trait in order for us to see it in another. The good news is the same principle holds true for the positive and lovely things we see in another—it too is a projection of what lies within ourselves.

When another person pushes our buttons, perhaps the gift they offer us is an invitation to practice tolerance, nonjudgment, or patience with ourselves. Have you ever felt intolerant of your own capabilities in some area of your life? I certainly have. Do you ever feel impatient with yourself? Oy . . . that is a hot button for me. When was the last time you looked in the mirror and judged yourself for being less than the perfect physical specimen you want to be? LOL! I won't even comment on that one. Suffice it to say, the egoic self doesn't like to attack itself so it will project our perceived shortcomings on others and use them as moving targets.

So, in response to the person who called in to the radio program asking how to deal with certain irritating, garden-variety, objectionable people, the answer is quite simple. While we may have to coexist with them at the workplace or even in our own home, we can mindfully choose to cease allowing them to push our buttons. How so? From a spiritual perspective, while we can't change other people, we certainly can change our perception of them. If you find that others are pushing your buttons too often, rather than reacting to them, consider taking a deep breath and silently thanking them for the reminder to pause and look within. For it is there, and only there, that you'll find the owner's manual for instructions on how to uninstall those buttons. In other words, inquire within and push "reset" by affirming "Everywhere I look I see the face of the Infinite One." In the process you'll be amazed at how it changes how you see yourself and, therefore, all of those beautiful souls who, up until now, have so effectively chafed your chaps.

HAPPY TRAILS, INDEED.

Is it possible to truly be immersed in perfection when the human condition is subject to so many things that appear to be far less than perfect?

The Sacred Practice of Being Perfectly Imperfect

> This Original Life is Infinite. It is good. It is filled with peace. It is of the essence of purity. It is the ultimate of intelligence. It is power. It is Law. It is Life. It is in us. In that inner sanctuary of our own nature, hidden, perhaps from objective gaze, nestles the seed, perfection.
>
> ~ ERNEST HOLMES, *THE SCIENCE OF MIND*

One of the blessings of living in Southern California is that I seldom have to drive to the market to buy citrus fruit because we have lemon, lime, and orange trees growing on our property. Recently, I went to gather a few lemons and I was not disappointed. Right there waiting to be picked, hung a plethora of perfectly packaged, beautiful, ripe and ready to use, tart treats directly from God's great garden. Then I saw it. I couldn't miss it because growing right in the midst of these beautiful lemons was one that was oddly different; compared to the other lemons it appeared to be deformed. After closer inspection it was obvious that this misshapen lemon was, in fact, several lemons that had somehow grown into one another, morphing into one, large, bulbous, bumpy, awkward looking piece of fruit. After picking it, my first inclination was to toss it because—not only did it appear far less than perfect—it was just plain unsightly. I thought, this one doesn't belong in the fruit bowl with all these other beauties. It was then that my inner voice gently nudged me saying, "Whoa! Judge not according to appearances—there is more here than meets the eye; take a breath and look for a deeper truth." It became obvious to me that this was the Universe inviting me to deepen my awareness that my eyes don't always report the truth. Too often our eyes are on a mindless mission to find fault with something rather than focusing on what is inherently right and good about it.

I took the misshapen lemon, along with a "normal" lemon, into the kitchen and cut both of them open. Beyond their outer form there was absolutely no difference. What lay at the *center* of the fruit was perfectly the same; the taste, color, and consistency of the juice and pulp were identical. The awareness I had was that, contained within seeds from both lemons was the *same* DNA which originated from a *single* source; the roots of one lemon tree. The essential "differences" in the lemons lay in my less than discerning eye, not in their essence. The lesson for me wasn't a new one because I have heard that inner voice before. I just needed another reminder of how easy it is to rush to conclusions based on appearances. Who knew my master teacher of the moment would be a lemon! There is a lesson here for all of us when it comes to remembering the perfection of the sole/soul source from which we have all originated.

When another master teacher, Jesus, admonished us to judge not according to appearance, he probably wasn't talking about lemons but nonetheless, the intent of his message is universal. He was guiding us to seek and unify with the source and sacred presence of perfection that is imbued in all things. Dr. Holmes points out the same principle in the opening quote. Hidden from our human eyes, beyond our objective (judgmental) gaze, deep at the center of all living things, lies a seed of perfection that knows no conditions. That seed is our spiritual DNA: the seed of Original Life, the perfection of God that was imbued in us the moment we were given the gift of life. It is we who are far too quick to jump to conclusions based on what our eyes report as imperfect. The only problem is, with that perspective, the inclination is to toss the best part of ourselves away, discounting ourselves as less than whole, not quite as good as others on the tree of life . . . and yet we *all* come from the same source—the same tree.

One of several definitions for the word *perfect* is, "absolute or complete." Because God is all there is, we are immersed in the Absolute perfection It is. To be complete means nothing is missing. To understand this wisdom is the beginning point from which we can learn to make peace with—and personalize—a universal principle that renders all things perfect even when they may appear otherwise. Understanding this principle invites us to embrace our humanity *and* our divinity simultaneously by seeing everything as *perfectly* imperfect. It's about reframing our concept of what "perfection" is and training ourselves to see it when and where others may not. The key is to think independently rather than being mesmerized by what Holmes referred to as "race mind," that subjective collective thought of the human race whose tendency is to think down, looking for what's wrong, rather than up, looking for what's right and good.

The Practice and Power of Seeing Beyond Appearances

Perhaps one of the greatest examples of seeing nothing less than the inherent perfection of Original Life within everyone, beyond all appearances, is found in the story of Jesus and the man with the so-called withered hand.

> And, behold, there was a man who had a withered hand. . . . Then says He to the man, stretch forth your hand. And he stretched it out . . .
>
> ~ MATTHEW 12:10, 13.

You'll notice that the great teacher did not say, "Oh, you poor soul, how sad you must be . . . that looks like it really hurts . . . what's in your consciousness to create this negative experience? Stretch forth that oddly misshapen hand." No . . . he said, "Stretch forth your hand," period. While others were busy perceiving a withered hand, Jesus was so focused on God's presence and perfection within (and as) the man, he *never* saw his hand as anything but whole. He was not seduced by the drama—he gave no power to the appearance, the story, or the consciousness of the man. He saw the Truth of the man's Being—he saw only the perfection of Original Life that lay within the man and affirmed it by saying stretch out your *hand,* fully believing he could and would. This is exactly what students and practitioners of Science of Mind are trained to do—to look beyond appearances. To not get caught up in the story. To know the Truth and declare it; to see the person as *already* immersed in a spiritual prototype of perfection, the Absolute perfection of Infinite Intelligence, and affirm that it is so, faithfully leaving the rest to the Law of Mind. In *The Science of Mind* Ernest Holmes writes, "What the healer does is to mentally uncover and reveal the Truth of Being, which is that God is in and through every man [human being] and that this Indwelling Presence is already Perfect. . . . Thought is sifted and that which does not belong to the real man [spiritual being] must be discarded." To help illustrate this point, I share one of my favorite stories about revealing the perfect being you *already* are. This is a brief excerpt from my book, *The Art of Being: 101 Ways to Practice Purpose in Your Life:*

> Perfection is finally attained not when there is no longer anything to add but when there is no longer anything to take away, when a body has been stripped down to its nakedness.
>
> ~ ANTOINE DE SAINT-EXUPÉRY

> As the apprentice gazed with amazement over the shoulder of the brilliant Michelangelo working on his masterpiece, the statue of David, he

> asked, "How will you ever create the perfection
> you seek from this slab of crude marble?"
> The master replied, "I have to add nothing
> because the perfection is already there.
> All I must do is remove the unnecessary pieces.
>
> ~ AUTHOR UNKNOWN

While I am not certain of the source of this story, or even if it is true, the moral of the message is one with which we can all relate. To find value in the lesson we must each personalize it and see where it may apply in our own lives. Where does "perfection" seem to be missing in your life? It depends on your perception. Removing the unnecessary pieces is the practice of a lifetime. To train ourselves to see only the presence and perfection of Original Life within ourselves and others and discard all thoughts and beliefs that may be shrouding the Truth of our Being may seem like a high calling. That is because we overcomplicate the practice. Understanding that our thoughts (backed by our beliefs) tend to become things, it helps to remember the practice is not a process of addition—it's one of subtraction. As Holmes infers, it's a process of mindfully sifting out and discarding thoughts that tell us there is something missing which must be added to who and what we are before we can be perfect, whole, and complete. As we discard those thoughts we naturally begin to see, as the great teacher saw, we are *already* immersed in perfection. Perfection, like wholeness, is not a condition—it is a state of mind and being. This is something to remember the next time we walk into a hospital or come upon a situation where conditions and appearances may overpower our senses. If God is all there is, could there be any less of God's presence and perfection there than say, a health spa or fitness club, or even a church, temple, or mosque? Of course, the answer is no.

The practice of seeing the presence and perfection of God at the center and circumference of our lives does not mean the experience we may be going through isn't real. It does not mean that there is no such thing as oddly misshapen lemons on the tree of our life. It means that we can take a step back and see it all through new eyes, knowing we are not alone and that we are one with something that is divinely perfect—something far greater than what our eyes report. Honoring and embracing our humanity with all our perceived flaws is a crucial component to living a life of wholeness. The practice is to remember that irrespective of where we are or what is happening, the Original Life that is God is there. That life is our life NOW and it is perfect just the way it is; it always has been and shall forever be.

This then is the sacred practice of being *perfectly* imperfect. We could say it's how we make perfect lemonade out of the imperfect lemons that may grow upon our tree of life. Now breathe and enjoy the moment.

IT REALLY IS PERFECT—JUST THE WAY IT IS.
AND SO ARE YOU.

Believing it is more blessed to give than receive is like believing it's more blessed to breathe out than in.

The Art of Receiving Is DIFFERENT from the Act of Taking

> Gracious acceptance is an art—an art which most never bother to cultivate. We think that we have to learn how to give, but we forget about accepting things, which can be much harder than giving . . . . Accepting another person's gift is allowing him to express his feelings for you.
>
> ~ ALEXANDER MCCALL SMITH

As many of my friends and readers know, in addition to Diane, who is my best friend, cheerleader, confidant and wife, my "other" best friend is of the four-legged variety. Mac Doodle is a seven-year-old, half Goldendoodle, half Labradoodle, eighty-pound bouncing ball of fluffy fur with a wagging tail at one end and a drooling tongue at the other. From the day we brought him home he has been the energetic embodiment of love; his devotion to Diane and me is at times humbling. Josh Billings was spot-on when he wrote, "A dog is the only thing on earth that loves you more than you love yourself." It just seems to be in a dog's DNA to give of himself fully to those he considers to be members of his pack.

I think we could all learn something significant from dogs regarding the nature of not just giving, but receiving. There seems to be sufficient conversation around the need to be a good giver, but little talk about the other end of the stick—the necessity of being a good receiver, which is where Mac comes in; he is not only a master at giving love and affection, he is also highly skilled at receiving it. From the day he was old enough to negotiate the stairs, every morning Mac's ritual has been to scamper down the stairs ahead of me and sit on the third (not the fourth or the second, but always the third) step from the bottom. There, he waits patiently for me to sit down next to him and give him a thorough scratch and massage from stem to stern. Only then will he come off the stairs and enter the kitchen where he enjoys his morning meal. While to some, this may sound like a dog with entitlement issues, I would have to disagree because dogs have no ego. I see it more as a statement of Mac's ability to naturally and fully receive as much nurturing, attention, and love as he gives. Therein lies the lesson for each of us.

Although the motives of how and why human beings give to others may differ from that of dogs, suffice it to say many of us are far better at the giving than the receiving. Let us be clear, there is a big difference between a "receiver" and a "taker." Takers are plentiful in our world—they "take" with no sense of propriety or desire to give anything in return, unless there is something in it for them. This is the mindset that often comes with a sense of entitlement, which is a mistaken belief that the world (or someone specific) *owes* them that which they are taking. Receivers, on the other hand, are open to what is being offered and are able to graciously accept it with gratitude and, if appropriate, humility. The difference between a taker and a healthy receiver comes down to self-worth: A taker takes because he has an agenda and most often, a consciousness established in lack and limitation; he simply doesn't feel worthy of receiving so he takes to ensure he has "enough." A receiver, on the other hand, accepts what is given because he knows he is worthy of receiving—and when appropriate and able, extends the giving, in one form or another, to others.

Knowing that we are all passengers traveling on that perpetual learning curve known as the road of life, I invite you to do try this Mindfulness Practice: Ask yourself, "On my daily journey and in my interactions with others (friends, family and strangers) do I tend to be more of a taker or a receiver?" One of the best ways to determine this is to first be mindful the next time anything is given to you. It could be something tangible such as a material gift, a meal, money, a ride, a job . . . or it might be something more intangible such as a compliment, having someone open a door for you or letting you into a busy traffic lane, getting directions from a stranger, a person's time, a smile, a hug, a kiss . . . In any case, whether the giving be tangible or intangible, examine your feelings and notice which emotions spontaneously arise from within. Are you simply "taking" what is being given for granted, or are you mindfully "receiving" it? The different energy between the two is palpable. After you locate the feeling, just sit with it. The way you'll know if you are a worthy receiver is that, irrespective of what is being given, a wave of gratitude, which is the natural reciprocal energy of life in motion, will rise up from within and wrap itself around you.

We don't have to be a dog to know the difference between "taking" and "receiving" and how one links us with the energy of life and the other separates us. Mindfully and gratefully receiving what is being given not only honors the giver—it honors us—it is a way of affirming to the universe that we know we are one with something infinitely larger than ourselves. Just as Mac does naturally, when we align with our true nature there is something within us that knows we are inherently worthy of receiving the best life has to offer.

AND IF THAT DOESN'T
MAKE OUR TAILS WAG, MOST LIKELY,
NOTHING WILL.

Have you ever wondered
what on earth God had in mind when placing
over seven billion soul beings on this precious, fragile,
beautiful blue pearl of a planet?

On a Mission from **God!**

> Love is a complete unity with life, and we cannot enter this state unless we are in unity with all that lives, for all life is One. To love God alone is not enough, for this would exclude our fellow man [human]. To love our fellow man alone is not sufficient, for this would be too limited a concept of God . . . When we realize that God and man are One and not two, we shall love both . . . We are to look for God in each other and love this God, forgetting all else.
>
> ~ DR. ERNEST HOLMES, *THE SCIENCE OF MIND*

Do you ever ask yourself why you were born? Your perspective regarding your presence on the planet is crucial because it determines the level at which you shall see your own life's purpose. Have you ever considered why there are so many people on the planet and why you—*specifically you*—are one of them? Perhaps the most salient and sacred question you can ever ask yourself is what is the meaning of this shared journey on what Buckminster Fuller referred to as Spaceship Earth?

From a human perspective this question may appear to yield one answer, while from a spiritual perspective something profoundly different may be unearthed. And yet the paradox is—in the end—that one perspective serves the other exquisitely well. So let us explore the question seekers that from antiquity have asked, Why have you come to earth?

The Paradox of Perspective

> "Non nobis solum nati sumus."
> (Not for ourselves alone are we born.)
>
> ~ MARCUS TULLIUS CICERO

To ask why we are here with seven billion other universal traveling companions is a sweeping question to ponder because with the right perspective, the answer can create an opening in our awareness that leads to a redefining moment for us as individuals, and what's more important, collectively as a species. And herein lies the paradox of perspective: Is it possible that we were put on this planet *with* one another *for* one another? Could it be that simple and yet that all-encompassing at the same time? Clearly, we need one another to procreate and co-create an infrastructure for living on the surface of life in order to exist as a species. However, if we are willing to go deeper, below surface living, our perspective may be altered.

What if we could see our time on the planet as a sacred sojourn—as if we are each soul beings here, as the Blues Brothers said, on a mission from God? What might that mission be—do you remember? As soul beings we knew why we were born on this blue pearl of a planet, but over the years, living on the surface of life in a human skin, we've forgotten the simplicity and beauty of that mission. Imagine the following scene:

You are on another dimension and yet without body or form. You have no personality, no gender . . . no identity with anything except an innate awareness that you are pure, unformed Heavenly Essence that has become individualized as a soul being. You are standing in a long line with millions of other soul beings, very patiently awaiting your divine assignment. Finally, you are given your task. You review the assignment and sign a contract stating your willingness to go on this mission from God. Your mission, in one respect, is unlike that of any other soul, and yet there is also a common element: You will be sent here for the "sole/soul" purpose of expressing your highest potential while at the same time, leaving the planet a better place than it was when you arrived. How you choose to do so is what makes your assignment uniquely yours. To assist you in completing your assignment you are given the body in which you live and certain innate gifts and talents that will make your mission meaningful and joyful. The excitement comes in learning what those gifts are and the joy comes in knowing it is never too late to use them to accomplish your mission.

Awakening from our spiritual amnesia will lead us to a deeper understanding of why we are all *together* on this planet. Perhaps that remembrance might even lead to the creation of a world that works for everyone—a world where reverence, selflessness, generosity, cooperation, loving-kindness, and compassion are the norm rather than the exception. Have we overcomplicated the answer to the question of why we are here because our perception of what gives life purpose and meaning has become a blurred, faded, ancient memory? Could the ultimate answer be so simple that we fail to see it because we are so close to it every moment of every day? Perhaps the resolution we seek through this flurry of questions is eloquently summarized in the hauntingly beautiful song/chant, "Love, Serve, and Remember" written and sung by my longtime friend Dr. John Astin:

> Why have you come to earth, do you remember?
> Why have you taken birth, why have you come . . . ?
> To love, serve, and remember . . .
> To love, serve, and remember . . .
> To love, serve, and remember . . .

While I have admired and sung John's song many times over the years, I had never asked him what inspired him to write it until recently. He told me, "Ram Dass would often tell the story of when he was getting ready to leave his guru [Neem Karoli Baba] in India and how he felt overwhelmed by the prospect of returning to 'the world,' unsure whether he'd be able to hold onto and integrate the profound insights he'd experienced while being in India. His teacher said to him, 'It's quite simple, just love everyone, serve everyone, and remember God.'"

John went on to say, "I always loved that story and the words sort of stuck in my mind for a number of years. Then one morning, while singing at a retreat in Hawaii, there was an absolutely spectacular sunrise. As I wandered the grounds gently singing to awaken those at the retreat, the chords to "Love, Serve, and Remember" started to come to me. And then very effortlessly the words just poured out. The song was born right then and there. That's the story . . . oh, as I sometimes like to share, it was also the first song I sang to my now nineteen-year-old daughter, just minutes after she was born."

Can you imagine how different our journey on Spaceship Earth might be if someone had sung this song to us when we were born? To love everyone, serve everyone, and remember God as a way of life may be "simple" but it's not necessarily easy—it is a high calling. It is a tall order for most of us because it seems to rub up against our "human" nature; that part of us that wants to put ourselves first and, often, above others. Perhaps we are overcomplicating the process. If we were to begin with the end in mind by remembering first and foremost, that the presence of God is *already* at the center and circumference of *all* that is, the actions of loving and serving *everyone* would be inherently simplified. Again, perspective is everything.

How Is It Possible to Love Everyone?

The ancients have long taught that we are each the living vessels through which and *as* which God loves Itself. What greater gift could we bring to our world? Might this be how the commingling of heaven on earth is manifest in the here and now? Can you wrap your mind around the idea that this is your mission, this is why you took birth: to "be" love and to *be loved*? Are you willing to venture deeply enough into the depths of your own sacred Self to embrace the simplicity of that idea? As simple as it is at the soul level, the human mind will argue that it is a *very* complex issue. Is it even humanly possible to love *everyone* . . . really? Even those whom you may not like? The egoic mind will come up with a multitude of reasons why it is not possible. Perhaps Ram Dass's teacher understood the quagmire and chasm that judgment creates between ourselves and others, which is most likely why he also threw in "and remember God" at the end of his admonition. The task is simplified by remembering God's presence. But what does that look like in real time?

When Dr. Holmes says we are to look for God in each other he was offering us an invisible bridge across that chasm—a sacred practice of the highest calling known as reverence. The practice is to remember that loving *everyone* doesn't necessarily mean making them our buddies and hanging out with them. It means seeing the sacred presence of the One behind *every* face and honoring that presence. Living with reverence allows us to see the manifestation of God *everywhere* we look—even in the face of those we may not humanly understand, like, or agree with. Reverence allows us to perceive and love that which is beyond action, personality, and form.

You Are Never Too Old or Too Young to Serve

> You have not lived today until you
> have done something for someone
> who can never repay you.
>
> ~ JOHN BUNYAN

Serving others comes with the role of being a whole human. When we live with reverence, serving others comes naturally with grace and ease. Why? Because our intention is not driven by the ego or from an expectation of receiving anything in return; we give, not to receive but to affirm we are one with Life. Selfless service is an action that arises from within the individual as a direct experience. It does a detour around the egoic mind. The intention that drives selfless service is singular; it connects hearts with hearts. This means we have no agenda whatsoever, other than to be a conduit through which the energy of unconditional love touches and lifts others, bringing a ray of light into their lives. That is what makes our service "selfless"—and it's never too soon or too late to realize this. As an example, I recall the day my wife, Diane, had a conversation with her then ninety-year-old mother. When Diane told me that her mom expressed a need to connect with hospice my first instinct was to react with a bit of panic. I said, "Oh, my gosh, what has she been keeping from us . . . is she not well?" Diane smiled and said, "No honey, you don't understand; she wants to be trained to serve as a hospice *volunteer*." With that,

I took a deep breath and chuckled. Then I began to reflect on the deeper meaning of her mom's desire.

This was really a statement about my mother-in-law's intention to announce to life that even at ninety years of age she was still vitally alive and had a gift to share with the world. I know that she had been in more than a fair amount of emotional and physical pain since she lost her beloved spouse of sixty-plus years to Parkinson's disease. Ever since his passing I believe she had felt a bit lost and possibly a sense of purposelessness and some unhappiness. I believe that her deeper wisdom self was sensing the essence of what Gandhi meant when he said, "The best way to find yourself is to lose yourself in the service of others." Sometimes when we are in pain the simple act of extending ourselves to others brings with it some instant relief, happiness, and even more, a rediscovery of purpose and meaning—an understanding that who we are and what we do with who we are matters. Serving others lifts us up and opens a portal through which we can step into a new awareness of what brings us happiness, meaning, and purpose, irrespective of our age.

> I don't know what your destiny will be,
> but one thing I know: the only ones among
> you who will be really happy are those who
> will have sought and found how to serve.
>
> ~ ALBERT SCHWEITZER

Speaking of the irrelevance of age when it comes to selflessly serving others and the happiness it brings, I recall the day I received a call from my then fourteen-year-old granddaughter, Cailin, and my then sixteen-year-old grandson, James, inviting me to come and watch a baseball game in which they were involved. They both held black belts in Taekwondo and excelled at sports, so I went expecting to see some spectacular action on the field, but what I saw take place at this game literally took my breath away. Even at their tender ages, they had discovered the profound meaning to be found in selfless service to others.

In Southern California, there is a local sports program called the Little League Challenger Division in which special needs kids play baseball. Ballplayers range in age from four to their early twenties, and they are challenged by a multitude of mental and physical disabilities. For each child on the field there was a "buddy" playing near them, assisting them if needed, but what is more important, cheering them on. (In actuality, it appeared that the buddies were having as much, if not more, fun than the kids they were serving.) James and Cailin were two of the buddies on the field and, along with some other teen buddies, assisted at every game of the season. James and Cailin were there because they *asked* to participate; no one had mandated their presence. I believe they were called to be there by the same inner voice that silently whispered to their great-grandmother, saying, "Who you are matters—you have a gift to share, irrespective of your age, and that gift is *your* presence, *your* caring, *your* time, *your* compassion and *your* love." The lesson for me is that it's never too soon *or* too late to learn how to serve. Whether you are fourteen or ninety, know that *you* matter.

So, why have *you* taken birth—are you beginning to remember your mission? Why have you come to earth along with seven billion other soul beings? The answer is elegantly simple: We need *one another* to honor and fulfill our mission. The good news is you need look no further than the next person you meet today to actualize and be the unique delivery system by means of which God loves and expresses Itself in a manner in which no other human being on earth can. That is how important you are to the Universe; you and I were put on this planet *with* one another *for* one another. Can you *see* how amazing that is and *you* are? You *really* are on a mission from God.

HOW COOL IS THAT!
YOU REALLY *do* MATTER.

Living in a human skin is not always easy.
Sometimes things happen that are difficult to live with.
Thus the saying, Perspective is everything.

Accepting **What Is**

Anything in life that we don't accept will simply make trouble for us until we make peace with it.

~ SHAKTI GAWAIN

While conducting a mindfulness retreat, I was asked a very provocative question that I thought might be of interest to many: "Recently I received a not-so-good diagnosis from my doctor. How do I deny (avoid getting caught up in) the condition I am told I must be very aware of at all times? Sometimes I feel the need for a good cleansing cry; however I worry about giving energy to the negative thought that stimulates this emotion. What can I do?"

Many who practice the power of positive thinking teach that we should turn away at the onset of a negative condition or situation because we give it more power by staring at it fearfully. Metaphysically this is a sound theory if one is deeply anchored in the belief, as spiritual masters from antiquity have taught, that while we may be "in" this world we are not "of" this world. In other words, while our physicality may be subject to the reality of the conditions we encounter in the earth realm, as spiritual beings we know there is a higher reality based in our oneness with the Divine to which we aspire that defines the perfection of who we really are. Another way to understand the difference might be to ask ourselves, "Are we human beings having a spiritual experience or are we spiritual beings having a human experience?" Of course the answer to both is yes! It's finding a reasonable balance between the two "realities" that confounds most of us. Because we are not all yet fully enlightened, the "not of this world" belief sets the bar very high for most of us, and it can cause much senseless suffering and guilt if we think it is the only way to approach the challenges we encounter on our earth journey.

I know of very few people who have not at one time or another had something dealt to them by life that they didn't plan on or expect, let alone deserve: a frightening medical diagnosis, a sudden change in a significant relationship, the loss of a lifetime career. The common thread that runs through all these may be the tendency to deny or avoid dealing with the "what is" that has been dealt to us. How do we embrace the "what is" in a manner that allows us to respond to it proactively, rather than staring at it fearfully and thus giving it more negative power? The first step is acceptance. This does not mean we have to like "what is"—it means being willing to see the apparent reality of the moment. It still may frighten us or frustrate us, but the practice is to breathe and be with it. This action alone will begin to recall some of the power we give to a condition or circumstance when we fearfully deny or resist what is in the moment.

The second step is to make space in our minds and hearts for the Power that is greater than us to be revealed and wrap Itself around us through contemplative and unifying prayer. Perhaps the most empowering way to do this is found in Reinhold Niebuhr's Serenity Prayer:

God, grant me the serenity to accept
the things I cannot change, the courage to change
the things I can, and the wisdom
to know the difference.

This prayer opens us to the courage to acknowledge "what is," and if appropriate, the guidance and inner knowing to navigate over, around, or through it with grace and ease. Divine surrender opens the portal to a deep sense of inner peace that allows us to begin to see the world through new eyes. In other words, mindfully accepting what is doesn't mean it is our destiny—it simply cracks open the door to a higher reality through which the sacred Light of the true Self shines in the present moment. This means that even if the condition or situation persists, we perceive it differently, which again recalls the power we may have temporarily given to the problem. When we mindfully partner with our Higher Power, we always have more authentic power. This act alone can initiate a whole new flow of energy surrounding the "what is," possibly becoming a new cause to a new effect. As the ancients would say, "As within, so without—as above, so below."

Let There Be Light
A Mindfulness Practice to Dispel Darkness

> Light gives of itself freely, filling all available
> space. It does not seek anything in return;
> it asks not whether you are friend or foe.
> It gives of itself and is not thereby diminished.
>
> ~ MICHAEL STRASSFELD

If you are like me, you probably have a few days of darkness now and then—you know, those days when for various reasons, it seems difficult to overcome that sense of separation from life, meaning, and purpose. I believe those times come to us all. That sense of void can arise from within in times of great loss, or sudden, unexpected, and perhaps unwelcome, change. Often those who are going through the grieving process experience periods of feeling isolated and shrouded in the shadows of sadness. Then again, sometimes that sense of darkness and separation seems to show up out of the blue for no apparent reason whatsoever.

Irrespective of how or why, the key is to try to stay as conscious and proactive as possible when emotional darkness sets upon us, rather than be swallowed up by it. Sometimes the tendency is to deny, resist, or otherwise try to avoid the darkness by numbing ourselves with substances or activities that divert our attention, thinking we can outlast the darkness, which only exacerbates the problem. Other times we might try to stand toe-to-toe with the darkness and attempt to push against it, as if we can sweep or chase it out of the room with a broom. The wisdom of the ages tells us that what we resist, persists; we only give it more power over us.

Teachers from many of the great faith traditions have taught that darkness is simply the lack of the awareness of the presence of light; that when light is introduced, darkness fades into the nothingness from which it came. Light has always symbolized the presence of Infinite Intelligence, God, Spirit, the Self, Presence, the Beloved, or any of the many other names humankind has used to describe the Life Force behind all creation. Regardless of how we refer to it, the important thing to remember is that this Life Force is always present, even in our darkest of times—we just have to remember it is there and call it forward in our interior awareness. We don't have to create the light—we have to reveal it. As it says in Genesis 1:3, "Let there be light and there was light." Let there be light—allow the light that is already there to reveal itself. We need only open to its presence. No struggle, no pushing or forcing, no denying or avoiding the darkness . . . just allow it to reveal itself from within.

When we remember the presence of Light in our mind and heart, it brings an awareness of our connectedness to life and all sense of separation dissipates, followed by an inner peace that brings balance and a renewed perspective. This is when we begin to see the moment through new eyes; eyes that can see beyond the darkness and into a new day where a revitalized spirit, mind, and body await us. This may sound easier said than done when we are immersed in emotional darkness, which is why we need not overcomplicate the process of remembering. If you resonate with these words, I invite you to experience a process that will help you internalize them. I offer you this mindfulness practice that over the years has pulled me out of that dark place more than once. I encourage you to do this slowly and mindfully, truly allowing yourself to open to the experience:

- Take an unlit candle with you into a dark room.
- Sit in the darkness for several minutes and breathe mindfully; allow yourself to feel immersed in the darkness. Think of that dark room as how you feel inside. If appropriate, you can associate that darkness with any challenge you may be currently experiencing in your life.
- Light the candle and watch how the flame casts a gentle glow that naturally dispels the darkness filling the room with a soft light. Again, think of the room as your interior being. Breathe in the light that so softly illuminates the room. Feel yourself internalizing the light and allow it to fill your inner being.
- Finally, bless whatever the darkness represents to you and let it go—surrender it unto the light. Be it grief, disappointment, resentment, or whatever—feel its release and the lightness of being that fills its void.
- As you bask in the light imagine that you have done nothing more than remember the radiant presence of the Beloved One in that sacred moment and allowed it to envelop your entire being. Thus the saying, Let there be Light.
- Note that you didn't have to chase the darkness away, struggle with it, bargain with it, curse it, or fear it . . . you simply had to call forward the presence of Light and in the process, the apparent darkness faded into the nothingness from which it came.

The practice is to remind yourself that in those unavoidable moments of darkness, which come with the privilege of living in a human skin, it is the nature of the Light to give itself to you unconditionally. You don't have to resist or push back the darkness—you just have to remember to light the candle—to let the light of the Beloved dispel the darkness. This then is how we gently lift ourselves into the knowing that while we may be "in" this world, we are not necessarily "of" this world.

ONE MOMENT . . . ONE THOUGHT . . . ONE PRAYER . . .
ONE CANDLE . . . ONE BREATH . . .
AT A TIME.

Too often we rush to a conclusion about others
that separates us
from a deeper part of ourselves.

The Deeper Meaning of **Compassion**

When we generate compassion for the difficult people in our lives, we get to see our prejudices and aversions even more clearly. It can feel completely unreasonable to make a compassionate wish for these irritating, belligerent people. To wish that those we dislike and fear would not suffer can feel like too big a leap. This is a good time to remember that when we harden our heart against anyone, we hurt ourselves.

~ PEMA CHODRON

Many years ago I heard one of my teachers tell this story about compassion. In these difficult times I think it's a great reminder for all of us.

Once upon a time, while swimming along a bottom of the lake, a school of fish paused to look up to see what all the commotion was about. What they saw above them was a single fish racing, jumping, and skipping in and out of the water. Then one fish in the school turned to another and said, "Look at that jerk . . . who does he think he is anyway, just dancing and skipping across the lake! What a show off . . . he is so weird; it's no wonder he is all alone out there." Of course, what they didn't see was the lure and barbed hook that was painfully embedded inside the mouth of the fish as he fought and pulled with every ounce of energy he had against the nearly invisible line which the fisherman was quickly reeling in.

At times we can be just like the school of fish in this little parable. Life is like one big lake in which we are all swimming and sometimes someone "hooks" our attention with his peculiar or outrageous behavior and we rush to judgment. We tend to make assumptions and reach a conclusion based on that judgment and then we build a case to support it. Without really knowing what possible pain might be going on inside that person's mind or body, too often we say (or think), "Oh, look at that '#*?&!%#', acting so moody and glum," or, "What a bum, he should just get a job," or, "What a chip he has on his shoulder . . . he is really out of touch with reality." While all the time, this person may be doing the best he can to simply make it through the day. It is quite impossible for us to know what others are going through. It's interesting to note that don Miguel Ruiz's *Four Agreements* seem to fit in here perfectly: "Be impeccable in your word . . . Don't take anything personally . . . Never make assumptions, and . . . Always do your best."

The sad truth is, we often judge our loved ones even more critically than strangers. It is a curious thing, isn't it? Marcus Aurelius wrote, "If you are pained by external things, it is not they that disturb you, but your own judgment about them. And it is in your power to wipe out that judgment now." Perhaps compassion and non-judgment would be an easier conclusion at which to arrive if we could remember that every person in our experience is serving as a perfect mirror that reflects back to us some aspect of our own character we may not choose to or can't see in ourselves. Many people avoid compassion, not because they are callous, but because of their own fear of the pain they see in others—it reminds them of their own vulnerability.

In its purest form the word *compassion* means "together with feeling." This means that when we enter into compassion we heal all sense of separation from one another and we allow ourselves, to the best of our ability, to enter into the other's pain—not to fix it or heal it, or even share in it, but simply to be there and allow the healing energy of our presence say, "You are not alone—I am with you." I believe this is what every person in pain, be it physical or emotional pain, truly longs for—to know they are not alone. Spiritually we are never alone because we are all One. Perhaps it's time to demonstrate that more fully in our lives. The only prerequisite for compassion is non-judgment and a willingness to share sacred space with another, if only for a few cherished moments.

Compassion heals in ways that medicine and empty words never will—at the level of the soul Self. This is an amazing gift we can bring into every relationship we shall ever have, from our most intimate others to the stranger across town. Let today be a day when you deepen your compassion and lessen your judgments. Your presence on this planet will make a difference if you can do this one simple thing.

YOU MATTER.

Can you imagine God
"spilling" Itself into a Divine template called "you"—
manifesting as spirit, mind, and body?

The Mystical **Marriage**

> The great mystics have been illumined. They have seen through the veil of matter and perceived the Spiritual Universe . . . All emerge from that One Whose Being is ever present and Whose Life, robed in numberless forms, is manifest throughout all Creation. Creation is the logical result of the outpush of Life into self-expression.
>
> ~ ERNEST HOLMES

As a dedicated student of ontology—the study of the nature of existence or being—I believe there is no more compelling quest upon which to embark than the journey back to our personal point of origin. Along the way we may begin to remember a vital part of ourselves we had long forgotten about: that mystical place within us where the Universe has personalized Itself. Inherent in every living thing is an insatiable hunger—the desire and power to push out—to express life by freely and fully being what it was uniquely created to be. To personalize this, consider the possibility that there was a time when you were a "what" before you were a "who." If you can conceive of that possibility, then the question to explore is, *what* were you before you became a *who*—and why did you become the *who* that you particularly are when there are so many other "who's" on the planet you might have been? This is the quintessential question that requires exploration if you are to find your way back to your true point of origin—and make no mistake about it—this is the spiritual sojourn you were born to make. In the process you may be led to fully understand the significance of your life and how important *you,* as an individual, really are to the Whole of Life. So let us consider where and when it all started.

About fourteen billion years ago the first chapter of the greatest miracle and mystery of all time began when something beyond all human logic and comprehension happened; the Ethers of that which for countless millennia would become known to humankind by many different names, began to stir. Because, as in any creative process, thought must precede form, Its first thought was, "I AM." This was the initiating sacred spark of Life; in a flash, self-igniting, giving birth to, and realizing the idea of Itself. In the process of unfolding from within and by means of Its own creative nature, It left, and continues to leave in Its wake, star-stuff—a living Universe that knows no restriction, only the impulse to eternally expand, perpetually becoming more of what It is, and can ever be . . . Life, expressing the "I AM" that It is, pushing out by creating Light and matter from *within* Itself, shaping and giving form *to* Itself—clothing Itself in an infinite and unique number of ways. Scientists might refer to this moment as the "Big Bang." Metaphysicians, on the other hand, might refer to it as the great "No Thing" becoming the great everything.

What does all of this have to do with you? Beyond the mystery of *how* the Universe gave birth to Itself, the deeper question lies in pondering *why* It gave birth to Itself and you. The answer can partially be found in the fact that you exist as a self-knowing being because you are a microcosm of the Divine Macrocosm—the only way the I AM can know Itself is in, through, and *as* Its creation. Ernest Holmes expounded upon this truth in *The Science of Mind* when he wrote, "We know by intuition, that there is something beyond what we have so far consciously experienced in this world . . . when the veil seems thin . . . Nothing can dislodge this inner and intuitive perception from our mentality . . . This is God in us knowing Himself." The ancients referred to the mystery of this miracle as the Mystical Marriage—the creation and union of an individual's unique soul-self with the Universal Soul-Self—and it happened the holy instant God conceived of and personalized Itself as you and me. However, the Mystical Marriage is not fully consummated until we *consciously* experience that union, which happens the moment we begin to remember from whence we originally came.

The journey back to your point of origin
is not really one of discovering who you are—
it's one of remembering who you are.

The role of your soul's invisible presence in the world is to be the Divine emissary of the universal I AM from which it came; its purpose is to circumnavigate the totality of your life, exploring the terrain of the human condition, gathering soul-expanding information through direct experience. From the depths of its innate connection to the Whole, it integrates itself with your body, which is simply a biodegradable vessel it commissions and occupies for the journey. Your soul seeks the Wholeness it knew before it landed in your body, where it instantly began to develop a severe case of spiritual amnesia, forgetting from whence it came by taking on all sorts of labels that reinforce the illusion of duality and separation. The "consummation" of the Mystical Marriage happens in that micro-moment of remembrance when we realize that, as Dr. Holmes put it, what we are looking for we are looking with. This is where and when the *what* and the *who,* which have always been one, fully merge in our awareness. The practice is to learn how to mindfully bring as much of the *what*-you-are into the expression of the *who*-you-are in the present moment. With a little bit of conscious intention this happens organically as the Essence of the intangible "Original Self" rises and commingles with the tangible "self" and ties the knot, unifying the two as one. In this process, the imagined line between the *what* and the *who* dissolves.

Suffice it to say, even though the Whole is greater than the sum of Its parts, the Whole is wholly contained within and *as* each part. Perhaps Dr. Holmes stated it more eloquently when he wrote, "The One encompasses and flows through All, spilling Itself into numberless forms, and personalities." That is quite a visualization, isn't it? Can you imagine God "spilling" Itself into a Divine template called "you"—manifesting as spirit, mind, and body? In addition, consider the fact that the template called "you" could be used only *once* for all of eternity; that is how unique you are *and* how important you are to the congruency and wholeness of an expanding universe.

Have you given much thought to why there are so many "who's" on the planet?

Knowing we are all emanations of the One, some say God is quite the trickster, doing it all with mirrors, and yet if you were to look closely at the seven billion "mirrors" currently occupying the planet, not one of us reflect exactly the same image. Why is this? Spiritually speaking there is no need for two of anything exactly the same because it would be redundant; although the Universe loves multiplicity and is infinitely prolific in individuated forms of expression, each one is unique and unlike any other. This is why living authentically is so important; it honors the purpose you are here to serve—to be you—and *no one else* can "do you" better than you can. This is equally important to remember when your life path intersects with other personalities by means of those interesting things we call relationships. Honoring other people's need to be uniquely who they are, rather than who we think they should be, is to honor the Divine intention imbued in them as they too arrived on the planet: to be a one-of-a-kind emanation of Light and matter tightly consolidated into a space suit called a body.

Why Conscious Relationships Matter

Our relationships are the vehicles for our evolution as individuals and a species. If we are fully conscious, our relationships offer us the clearest view of our own souls because they invite us to look directly into the face of the Divine and see our own reflection. We all desire relationship—where someone is there to witness our life and to reflect back to us the truth that who we are matters. This is the spiritual component that drives our deep desire for connection with other human beings, even if we are not consciously aware of it. The paradox is, out of the One, the many are manifest and drawn together to remind ourselves that we are not alone—that we, individually, and collectively, are part of something far greater than ourselves. Taking poetic license I respectfully paraphrase what a great teacher once said: Where two or more are gathered . . . there too is the I AM. Something extraordinary happens between ourselves and others when our lives intersect at the soul level. Be it our significant other, family members, friends, coworkers, or even strangers; with a remembrance of the One Central Flame that sent us forth as divine sparks we can consciously come together with others with reverence—knowing we are connecting with not just a physical body covered with labels, or a personality, but the very Essence of Life. This is when we are reminded that the mirror of Oneness has many reflections and each one is no less sacred than another. As Dr. Holmes inferred, this is God spilling Itself into numberless forms and personalities by means of every relationship we have. There is something within each of us that knows this is true, and this is why we are compelled to seek a deeper connection with others—it reminds us of Home; the place of Oneness from whence we have come and to which we are destined to return as we trace our lineage back to the source of our origin. The homing beacon is eternally wooing us, trying to get our attention. If you pay attention to your subtle energy right now you'll notice something stirring within you, nudging you to come closer. This is the I AM "*re*-calling" you—calling you back to wholeness, reminding you of your point of origin—reminding you of *who* you truly are, and even more important, *why* you are. The fact that you are reading this book is an indicator that you are starting to listen to the call.

As a mindfulness practice consider stepping outside on a clear night and gazing up to the stars—and think about the billions of galaxies beyond them. Take a deep breath and imagine back...back...way back, to that singular sacred second before anything existed. Then contemplate, out of the void, the great "No Thing" self-igniting, becoming the great everything, unfolding Itself, knowing only Itself as I AM, perpetually becoming the All that is at the speed of light. Finally, realize that was the moment the idea of "you" was conceived in the mind of God; it just took this long for you to arrive here because timing is everything. You are here *now* because you are supposed to be here. Just as it can take tens of thousands of years for the light of a distant star to reach Earth, the *what*-you-are arrived on the planet to became the *who*-you-are at precisely the right moment. You are a Divine idea in the mind of God whose time has come to shine. The veil has been pulled back, the Mystical Marriage has taken place, and now it's time for you to attend the reception because the party just wouldn't be complete without you—you matter.

AND I MEAN THAT LITERALLY.

Your life is shaped by the choices you make.
Are you making them wisely?

Conscious **Choice**

Man is made or unmade by himself. By the right choice he ascends. As a being of power, intelligence, and love, and the lord of his own thoughts, he holds the key to every situation.

~ JAMES ALLEN

As a spiritual mentor, part of my job is to challenge the people I work with to consciously observe their BS (belief system) and challenge any current beliefs they hold that are keeping them stuck in a mental prison of their own making. The moment is quite interesting to witness when they discover that they, and they alone, hold the key that will set them free. The key, of course, is their ability to choose and then choose again if necessary. When they awaken to the awareness that they can witness their own thinking, and then challenge the thoughts that are disempowering, nonproductive, and self-deprecating (and the beliefs that sponsor those thoughts), this is the moment they step into a whole new way of being.

One day I upset a person I was mentoring when I challenged her to look at her belief system after she argued she "just couldn't" do something I had suggested she might consider trying to fortify her spiritual growth. I encouraged her to begin to monitor her thinking and words, and each time she caught herself declaring, "I can't," to stop, challenge her belief, and then change the statement to, "I choose not to." I explained to her that to say "I choose not to" put her at the center of her authentic power, while to say "I can't" rendered her powerless.

This shift in thinking and words automatically moves us out of powerlessness and into a position of authentic power and choice. There are, no doubt, many legitimate times when we may be unable to do something because we are not capable. As an example, I can't fly a F18 fighter jet . . . I can't give birth to a baby . . . I can't lift 750 pounds over my head, and so on. However, too many of us rush to use the excuse "I can't" because it is far easier than having to deal with the possible consequences of saying, "I choose not to." Notice how often we tend to sacrifice our authentic power and integrity just to gain or maintain the approval and acceptance of others. This is where we can choose to step into our truth. Consider in your own life how often you may use "I can't" as a cop-out. Have you ever been asked by someone to do something or go somewhere you really did not want to do or go, and said, "I'm sorry, but I can't," perhaps even fabricating some excuse rather than honestly saying, "No thanks, I choose not to."

Regardless of what your motivation may be for using the "I can't" escape clause, I encourage you to be conscious of the power in your spoken word. The universe takes what you affirm about yourself very seriously—it conspires to support you in your deepest beliefs. You may end up more powerless than you would care to be. Think before you say "I can't" because every choice you make moves you closer to or further away from your authentic power. It is also how we spiritually evolve with conscious intention. In his seminal book, *The Seat of the Soul,* Gary Zukav states, "Choice is the engine of our evolution...if you choose unconsciously, you will evolve unconsciously. If you choose consciously, you will evolve consciously." Suffice it to say, choosing to evolve consciously is much better than unconsciously, and most often far less painful. Trust me...been there, done that.

As you begin to make conscious choices,
your life shall follow the trajectory
of those choices even as your shadow faithfully
follows you wherever you go.

The power of choice is the greatest gift you have been given, second only to the gift of life itself. Use both of these gifts consciously. In so doing, you will be stepping into your authentic power. If you could use a little help, as a mindfulness practice consider doing this: Place a rubber band (not too tightly) around your wrist. Listen to your words and self-talk for the next few days. When you catch yourself saying "I can't," when in actuality, you know in your heart you can, snap the rubber band. Then step into your power, making a choice to use words that reflect the awareness of a conscious evolving being. To say “I choose not to” rather than “I can’t” brings an amazing amount of authentic power and freedom with it.

AND AS A HAPPY RESULT THE WELTS ON YOUR WRIST WILL BEGIN TO SUBSIDE. ☺

Going with the flow means trusting life in the moment and letting go, knowing that you are part of something much larger than yourself. Can you trust life that much?

Honor **The Rhythm** of Life

We too often leave our souls behind. Caught up in urgency, we forget what is truly important in life. Pushed on by the demon of haste, we forget our souls—our dreams, our warmth, our wonder. From this viewpoint, it is clear how patience is a part of kindness, for how can we be kind if we do not respect the rhythm of others? We forget the soul—theirs and ours. The next time you surprise yourself while hurrying your child, or pacing up and down waiting for a late train, or forgetting to breathe in your haste, ask yourself where you left your soul. Kindness has a slow pace.

~ PIERO FERRUCCI, *THE POWER OF KINDNESS*

A while back I gave a discourse on the importance of feeling the rhythm of life and aligning with its flow, and it brought back fond memories of a journey through France that my wife, Diane, and I had taken. I returned to my home turf after that trip only to discover that a part of me was still in France and is yet today. The part of me I left behind (metaphorically, of course) is my soul. It is not at all that I don't love being back home, it is simply the fact that I really got into the rhythm of a different culture—a culture that honors the need for the soul and body to be in sync and harmony with life. It seemed that within twelve hours of my return home, my body and mind were once again running far ahead of my soul. I then became aware that there is still more for me to learn regarding the rhythm of my life.

I found it interesting that before I left for France, a number of people admonished me to "be ready for an experience with brash people who don't like Americans." The only thing I can report to you is that we drove over 2,400 kilometers, from one end of France to the other, and never had even one such encounter. If anything, our experience was laced with kind people. The French people were friendly and on more than one occasion, very helpful in giving us directions (including a map drawn on the wrapping for a baguette ~ truly). Language differences didn't seem to get in the way of heartfelt communications. Kindness seemed to be extended to us at every turn.

Make a Conscious Decision to Merge with What Is in the Moment

I would like to think that was because Diane and I are such exceptional people they all instantly loved us, but that wasn't the case at all. The only thing we did was observe the rhythm of the culture and make a conscious decision to merge with it rather than push against it or try impose our American rhythm on them. By rhythm, I mean how they "do" life—how life flows in their culture. As an example, we rented a car, which alone was an interesting way to experience their culture. Learning to let go of my expectations of when and how traffic should flow through the roundabouts and one-way streets, I just put the pedal to the metal and did my best to stay up with the crowd. It was amazing how everyone just sort of merged in a lane-less unity of one massive flow of traffic—a perfect harmonious blend of bicycles, motor scooters, Renaults, and trucks . . . and us. It was an interesting dance of energy to become part of, and I have to admit, it was more of an adrenaline rush than any ride at Disneyland. I continually reminded myself of the old adage, "Never drive faster than your guardian angel can fly." No doubt, our angels were on duty while we drove.

While in France, Diane and I did our best to live as the French live. We commingled with the rhythm of the culture and began to really enjoy the differences. The hours the French sleep and dine are far different from "ours"; the food they eat is considerably different from "ours." There everything is freshly prepared and the closest thing to fast food is a baguette strapped to the handlebars of a bicycle. The pace, while energetic, was never rushed. I am reminded of the Rumi quote, "Ever since happiness heard your name, it has been running through the streets trying to find you." Truer words have never been spoken, but we have to slow down a bit so our bliss, our happiness, can catch up with us. In my estimation, the French people have mastered the art of slowing down and enjoying the moment, which includes sharing it with even their pets as part of the family unit—even in restaurants.

Without question, the French are not wound nearly as tight as most of us. They give themselves ample time for eating and connecting with one another . . . and I noticed they laugh a lot. Perhaps that is because of the ever-present wine being served, but I think it is far more than that. I think they enjoy the moment because their souls are in alignment with their bodies. As one Frenchman told us, "Life in France is not about the quantity of our possessions but the quality of our lives. We value our relationships and the time to enjoy them." Perhaps we came across no "brash" people because we didn't expect to come across them. Then again, perhaps it was because we let go of any attachment to imposing our rhythm of life on them. Perhaps it was because we really had a chance to allow our souls to catch up with our bodies. Perhaps it was all the above.

How about you? Are you sensitive to your own rhythm and how it may differ from the rhythm of others? Are you giving your soul a chance to catch up with you on a daily basis? You don't have to travel halfway around the world to be reminded how important it is to honor the rhythm of life—both yours and other people's as well. Be kind to yourself and be kind to others by honoring the rhythm of life.

YOU DESERVE IT
AND SO DO THEY, OUI?

From antiquity, spiritual masters have taught that we are on a spiritual journey every moment of our lives. The practice is to remember there is not a spot God is not.

Mindfulness Matters

If you miss the present moment, you miss your appointment with life. That is very serious!

~ THICH NHAT HANH

Even before we took human birth our soul Essence was well on the journey to what would ultimately become our life on this planet. As mentioned in a prior chapter metaphorically, before we were sent here, God told each of us, "Your purpose is to go to planet Earth and Be me . . . and by the way, soon after your arrival you'll begin to forget who you really are and from whence you came." On the day of our birth our Essence was instantly squeezed into a very small, dense, physical container called a body and labels were immediately stuck on us such as gender, ethnicity, name, and so on. As we aged, even more labels were placed on us until we indeed did begin to forget who we really are and why we were sent here. Our focus became living up to, or in some cases, down to, the labels that defined us in the world. Then for many of us, one day something triggers a remembrance of that ancient conversation with the Beloved and we begin to recall that our sole/soul purpose is to "Be" the living manifestation of the One on this planet. In that moment of awakening we begin peeling away the labels and the journey takes on a new significance. As we remember who we really are and from whence we came, we become aware that we each are the One who brings heaven to earth every day in all we think, say and do. Mindful living is the art and practice of *remembering to remember* who we are on this journey.

Mindfulness is the process of being present in the moment with "what is" and allowing it to be your experience. It's being discerning enough to see through the dark cracks and crevices of the human condition and perceive the sacred Light therein. Suffice it to say, mindful living is a lifestyle—it's a way of consciously walking a sacred earth, incorporating purpose and an awareness of God's presence in all we say, think, and do on our journey of a lifetime. As we awaken to our soul's purpose, we inherently know that it is found in our daily experience. In other words, our reason for existing is right in front of us every moment of every day—it's being the vessel through which, but what is more important, as *which* the Infinite finds fullness of expression in an individualized manner.

The challenge for most of us is that our minds are often somewhere other than in the present moment. The day we were born, life became a linear process where we learned "doing" was very important and "time" became a commodity. This is when we began to forget who we really are. We were taught how to project ourselves into the future so we might one day create a life of meaning and purpose by accomplishing one goal after another, moving from one grade to the next, getting through school, acquiring a job, finding a partner, creating a home and so on—essentially acquiring even more labels as we went along. Indeed, we learned how to "do" life very well on this linear pathway, and in the process, most of us forgot how to "Be." Some say time is moving so fast that having a spiritual experience is very challenging—there's so much to do. In actuality, time is standing still because it's always now—it is we who are moving so quickly through time. Living mindfully can slow us down and bring us consciously and intentionally into the present moment, which is where we find our spiritual experience *waiting for us* to open to Its greatest gift—the peace that passes all understanding.

Right now, if we intentionally take a deep breath and focus on that breath we will discover that our mind and our body are in the same place at the same time. The irony is, one's body can't be any place other than in the present moment, but far too often one's mind is elsewhere. Mindfulness is the practice of calling the thinking mind back to the body so that the two become as one in the present moment. As we incorporate our awareness of God's presence in that moment, our doing becomes infused with our Being as *the activity at hand.* At this level of mindful living our every action becomes a spiritual experience, be it driving the car, mowing the lawn, changing the baby's diaper, selling real estate, performing brain surgery, or making love to our significant other. In other words, as we deepen our consciousness to fully embody the practice of mindful living, all of life becomes a sacred continuum.

Mindful living reminds us of the blessings in the moment we sometimes forget to see.

Isn't it amazing how often we don't take time to truly appreciate something until it is gone? We get complacent and slip into a "take life for granted" mode. This happens many times in relationships and often with our material status, but even more so with our physical well-being. Buddhist monk Thich Nhat Hanh writes, "When we have a toothache, we know that not having a toothache is happiness. But later, when we don't have a toothache, we don't treasure our non-toothache. Practicing mindfulness helps us learn to appreciate the well-being that is already there."

As a mindfulness practice, consider taking five minutes and write down some of the "non-problems" you have in your life *at this moment.* When was the last time you appreciated your heart and liver for the great job they do at keeping you healthy and alive? How about your feet and toes? (Did you know you would fall flat on your face without your toes?) How about your eyes and ears? What about the roof over your head; do you ever take your home for granted? Then move on and contemplate the relationships you have with your partner, family, and friends that give deep meaning to your existence. Would this be a good day to call someone you love and tell them so? Mindfulness helps us *remember* to remember to come back to the present and appreciate the blessings of the moment. Don't wait until you have a toothache to be appreciative of how good a "non-toothache" feels. Don't wait until your co-worker has gone home to say "good job." Don't wait until a loved one is no longer there to say "I love you." Don't wait until you have "time" to be mindful. Every moment is the time.

How to Calm the Waters of a Turbulent Mind

The mystical Sufi poet Rumi writes, "Only let the moving waters calm down, and the sun and moon will be reflected on the surface of your being." The waters of a turbulent mind will never reflect the light Rumi refers to, which is a metaphor for God's presence. Our minds are always moving here and there, most often lingering in either the happenings of the past or the concerns of the future where we have no power. The question is, what can we do to calm the waters of a turbulent mind in the present moment? For many of us, the waters of our daily life are anything but calm because we don't create space to experience the inner silence that can only be accessed through conscious breathing. When we stop to consider it, breathing is the most life-essential thing we do, and it is always a present moment experience. However, seldom are we consciously aware that we are breathing. When we pause and breathe mindfully, we open the portal to the Presence and enter a sacred silence where the waters are always calm.

Begin by breathing consciously and listen to the silence between breaths.

Breathing in, I calm my body.
Breathing out, I smile.
Dwelling in the present moment
I know this is a wonderful moment.

~ THICH NHAT HANH

Below is a mindfulness practice I invite you to try by using a silent mantra coupled with a breathing exercise:

- On a slow in-breath (focusing solely on the breath) silently affirm "God is," then gently hold that breath for approximately six seconds while mindfully observing the space created by non-breathing.
- Then on a slow out-breath of ten seconds, silently affirm "I am," and do not draw another breath in for six seconds while mindfully observing the space created by non-breathing.
- Repeat the cycle in a rhythm for five minutes (longer, if possible) silently affirming "God is . . . I am" and notice how a sense of inner peace rises in the field of your awareness and the waters are calmed.

Why Mindfulness Matters

There is no area of our lives where mindful living will not benefit our well-being . . . and our world. Our physical bodies and the body of our affairs literally vibrate at a higher frequency when we are mindful of God's presence. When we are guided to eat our meals mindfully, remembering the Source from whence it comes, food becomes a blessing to our body temple and we make wiser choices regarding what we put into it. Our relationships thrive when we are mindful of the presence of God because reverence and loving kindness become the practice with those with whom we interact. Likewise, at the workplace mindful living blesses all of those with whom we work or serve—when we are aware of Presence, every transaction becomes a sacred act and every product, customer, and employee is blessed by our "remembering to remember." Lastly, when we enter into each day remembering that abundance is the natural out-picturing of one who lives mindfully, aware of his or her connection and unity with Source, we tend to be more generous with our material good.

Mindful living is a simple concept to grasp—in the words of Ram Dass, "Be here now." However, in application mindful living may require a bit more effort because our thinking mind is so easily seduced by the vortex of a world obsessed with doing rather than Being. I recall one of my teachers saying, "Realization, without application, is hallucination." In other words, "Put your money where your mouth is, and stop dreaming about it."

The practice is to skillfully make mindful living a lifestyle. If all we do is gain an intellectual understanding of how to live mindfully but never apply it in our daily lives we shall never know the amazing gift the present moment holds for us. The gift, of course, is the richness of a life lived in the presence of the Beloved.

In short, mindful living blesses each of us and our world. Living mindfully makes every relationship sacred, every challenge on our pathway a stepping stone rather than a stumbling block, and every day an opportunity to live with a sense of awe, meaning, and purpose. The journey of our soul really is the journey of a lifetime and it's a journey we get to take whether we are aware or not. Mindful living brings awareness to the journey and frees us from the limitation of the labels that have defined us from the day we were born. With this in mind, let us "remember to remember" that who we really are and what we do with who we are truly matters.

May your journey through this day and every day be a conscious one where the intention of your soul intersects with the intention of your human nature on a daily basis, bringing your Being into alignment with your doing every moment of your life. That is what it means to experience heaven on earth.

YOU DESERVE IT—
AND SO DOES OUR WORLD.

Knowing the difference between a problem and an inconvenience makes every day of life a more meaningful experience.

The Blessing of Your Inconveniences

> One of life's best coping mechanisms is to know the difference between an inconvenience and a problem. If you break your neck, if you have nothing to eat, if your house is on fire, then you've got a problem. Everything else is an inconvenience. Life is inconvenient. Life is lumpy. A lump in the oatmeal, a lump in the throat and a lump in the breast are not the same kind of lump. One needs to learn the difference.
>
> ~ ROBERT FULGHUM

Last month I was living in what I referred to at the time as computer hell. Between changing Internet service providers (a bundle package including Internet, TV and phones . . . oyy), moving my website to a new server, email data base malfunctions, connectivity challenges between my printers, phones, and televisions, and downloading the latest software to update the operating system on my commuters, I spent more time talking to tech people than anyone else. Let's just say, it was a very challenging month dealing with one problem after another.

Then I ran across the quote by Robert Fulghum, and it sort of sucked the wind out of my sails and my iceberg of problems instantly dissolved into a puddle of minor inconveniences. The fact that we have so many wonderful things in our lives to be inconvenienced by is a true gift: computers, phones, cars, jobs, home maintenance and repairs. We could also include those minor aches and pains and even many of the challenges in our relationships with friends and family. In other words, unless you are on your way to the hospital, or living on the street and have nothing to eat, a detour on the road called "your daily life" is not so much a problem—it's an inconvenience.

Remembering how blessed we are by our "inconveniences" seems to be a lesson that most of us, including me, need to be reminded of on a regular basis. Speaking of the ongoing detours life puts in front of us, this past weekend while returning from a speaking engagement in Las Vegas and eager to get home, Diane and I became stuck in a major freeway traffic jam—cars were backed up and at a standstill for miles. At the time I saw it more as a problem than an inconvenience because I had consumed several cups of coffee, a coke, and a bottle of water and was particularly in need of a restroom. Eventually every car was sloooowly directed off the freeway and detoured through a number of side streets. As it turned out, the cause of the backup and detour was a brushfire along the freeway. It was only then that we learned there had just been a flash flood in the high desert area we had passed through which severely damaged a number of homes and automobiles. Diane was quick to remind me (and rightfully so) that given all that had transpired that day, I did not really have a problem; I was merely being inconvenienced and she was correct.

Everything is relative to our current experience and our perspective of it. The differences between our problems and our inconveniences become even more obvious when we consider the incomprehensible pain and suffering of the men, women, and children all around the world who are caught in the middle of warring nations, or famine and lack of clean water. I don't bring all of this up to cause us to feel guilty about how blessed our lives may be—I bring it up as a reminder that perspective is everything. As Robert Fulghum reminds us, one needs to learn the difference between an inconvenience and a problem, because in so doing life not only becomes more manageable, it becomes more meaningful.

If you are so inclined, the question I would invite you to do some self-inquiry around today is this: Where in your life might you have mistaken an inconvenience as a problem? Taking time to put things in proper perspective is a wise thing to do. The practice is to learn the difference between your inconveniences and problems, and appreciate them: just consider how blessed you are to have so many inconveniences and so few problems. If you do, when a true problem does show up, you will be able to recognize it and mindfully respond to it rather than mindlessly react to it.

BLESS YOUR INCONVENIENCES TODAY,
MY FRIENDS.

The word "Grace" is exquisite
because it can be defined, and thus experienced
in an infinite number of ways.
What does the face of Grace look like to you?

The Many **Faces of Grace**

> Now is the time to know that all that you do is sacred. . . . Now is the time for you to deeply compute the impossibility that there is anything but Grace.
>
> ~ HAFIZ

As we mature chronologically and spiritually, our understanding of what grace is and how it applies to our lives evolves. For many of us we need look no further than the dinner table for our original understanding and experience of grace. I recall as an eight-year-old child, sitting around the dinner table with my family, eyes closed, holding hands, saying grace in perfect unison. At the time, this action seemed little more than a perfunctory, memorized incantation, thanking an invisible sky God for the meal we were about to ingest.

In hindsight, however, I can see my parents were really quite brilliant—they knew exactly what they were doing. They fully understood that grace was far more than a perfunctory ritual—it was about grooming a consciousness of "conscious connection." Dinner was the only time of the day when our family of six could all be together at the same time and that time for connection was the glue in our home that bonded us with one another—and it is a bond which still holds to this day. As I matured and found my own spiritual path, grace took on a new face—a different form—and its meaning deepened, becoming the portal for a different kind of connection—a sacred connection. I grew to learn that grace is more than uttering certain words that connect us *to* God; it's something that, with unclouded perception, we can feel moving within and all around us in real time, unmistakably knowing it as the presence of God. This is when the word *Grace* becomes a proper noun because it is another name for God. Whether we can see it with our physical eyes at the time or not, when we are fully conscious, Grace is what we *experience* when all perceived separation from God has fallen away—and this can and does happen in a heartbeat. As odd as it may seem, it is often in the most dire of circumstances that people report feeling the Grace of God moving through them without their expecting or praying for it to happen.

It can be a humbling experience when we open to the idea that Grace is given to us regardless of whether we expect it or believe we deserve it. God's Grace cannot be earned—if it could, that would imply it could also be taken away, which is an impossibility. The gift of God's Grace is irrevocable because by Its very nature, God as a universal principle is omnipresent, nonjudgmental, and unconditionally giving. It is when we assign a personality to God, which is sometimes gentle, loving, and giving, and other times judgmental and punitive, that we mistake God's Grace as a favor for which we must compete, petition, grovel, or win by means of ornately pious behavior. This is clearly not the kind of God Ernest Holmes wrote about in his definition of Grace in *The Science of Mind:*

> Grace is the givingness of Spirit to Its Creation . . . but we need to recognize it. It is not something God imposed upon us, but the logical result of the correct acceptance of life and a correct relationship to the Spirit. We are saved by Grace to the extent we believe in, accept, and seek to embody, the Law of Good.

Few of us may have ever thought of Grace as the "Law of Good" in action but that is an empowering idea to wrap our minds around. Along with being a proper noun, this is when Grace becomes a verb as well. The point Dr. Holmes is making is that we don't have to beg, bargain, or grovel for the Grace of the Beloved because God is constantly *giving* all of Itself to Its Creation *all the time.* The only caveat is that we must be willing and able to identify and align with this Law of Good by opening to and *accepting* the gift that Grace brings—*and therein lies the rub.* Sometimes it can be extremely difficult to see what Holmes refers to as the "Law of Good" in the middle of what appears to be nothing less than something really bad. Often our faith, or lack of faith, in God's presence is too easily seduced by appearances because most of us have been conditioned to believe that

Grace only comes gift wrapped as love and light, clouds miraculously parting, and angels singing on high in three-part harmony. The deeper spiritual truth is that the faces of Grace are numerous —It can come upon us wearing many different disguises—some of which may not always look the way we might prefer.

Such was the case for spiritual teacher Ram Dass who in February 1997 suffered a devastating stroke. In a video documentary titled *Fierce Grace,* filmed a few years later, he remarks, "This isn't who I expected to be. Stroke, Grace, stroke, Grace, stroke, Grace—this has been my major spiritual exercise; bringing these two things together." He goes on to say, "I felt this was a terrible, terrible thing . . . the stroke caused me to lose my faith—and it was a cold, cold place—and I suddenly realized it was fierce Grace because it was one Grace that turned my life around." At another point in the interview, crediting the Grace he found in being "stroked," he states, "There are qualities in me that would have never come out."

My sense is that Ram Dass was humbly, consciously, and courageously reconciling his humanity with this divinity and in so doing, found himself entering the sacred portal to a redefining moment. This was when he realized that the Grace which opened the door to his transformation truly was fierce because the door wasn't gently opened—it was brutally kicked open in an extremely painful and completely unexpected way. And yet it was, nonetheless, by his own admission, the Grace needed to serve him in his continued evolution as a human being and a spiritual being. Suffice it to say, when we can see and *accept* it as a blessing, fierce Grace imbues us with the courage to stand face-to-face with "what is" and dance with it. Again, it's about conscious connection: when we enter this dance consciously and embrace Grace with the tenacity to not let go until we receive its blessing, we invariably draw something good from it.

To bless anyone or anything is to confirm
the presence of God at the
center of that which is being blessed.

Regardless of the different ways in which Grace reveals Itself to us, when we can consciously see, welcome, and embrace It, we may rest well in knowing we are receiving God's blessings. This is what it means, not only to "say" grace but to witness Grace activated in every area of our daily lives—in our homes, meals, bodies, relationships, careers, on our planet, and beyond. This is why it is important to develop a mindfulness practice of blessing everyone and everything in our lives. Grace is showering Its gifts upon us continually, but as Dr. Holmes reminds us, Grace is not something that is imposed upon us; *we must enter into Its presence* wherein It patiently awaits our arrival and acceptance. The practice is to mindfully accept life as it is in the moment, while continually *moving toward a deeper relationship with Spirit,* even when, on the surface, God's Grace appears to be awkwardly missing. As an example, in the following excerpt from poet David Whyte's beautiful book, *Crossing the Unknown Sea*—the metaphor is obvious: "You are like Rilke's Swan in his awkward waddling across the ground . . . moving toward the elemental water, where he belongs. It is the simple contact with the water that gives him grace and presence." Likewise, it is by the simple contact with our elemental Spirit, where we belong, that the Grace and presence of God reveal Itself, and our lives are transformed. Again, conscious connection is the conduit through which Grace flows into our lives in a multitude of ways —the faces of Grace are many.

A mystic is one who senses the Divine Presence.

~ ERNEST HOLMES, *THE SCIENCE OF MIND*

Have you ever thought of yourself as a mystic? If you are working at consciously living in the flow of God's Grace you might just be a mystic in training, and therefore, you could consider this your clarion call to mindful living. The practice is to be present in the moment with "what is" by realizing you are *already* swimming in the spiritual element in which you belong —Divine Presence. When we merge with God's presence in the present moment we lose ourselves in a flow of energy that tends to dissolve the imaginary line between where we end and God begins—this *is* Grace wrapping Itself around us as it does all living things. To see a hawk soar effortlessly on the thermals overhead without ever moving its wings is to witness Grace in flight. To watch a dancer glide with abandon and such fluidity that she seems to defy gravity is to witness the seamless energy of Grace in motion. It is fierce Grace that sustains a butterfly as it struggles to free itself from the cocoon of its own making, giving it the strength needed to express a newfound life with wings. Grace is the eternality of life forever flowing. Grace is what we see in the eyes of an infant as she draws her very first breath, or an elder's eyes as he releases his very last. And it is that same Grace that spans the sacred continuum between those two events which blesses and sustains us always, in all ways. We simply need to awaken to Its presence and accept the gift that has already been given.

Life gets no more mystical than when we consciously live in Grace. This is when the words of Hafiz ring ever more true: "*Now* is the time to know that all that you do is sacred . . . *Now* is the time for you to deeply compute the impossibility that there is anything other than Grace." No doubt, there are many, many faces of Grace. From the simple meals we mindfully share with others, to the Divine Impulse that animates all of life, Grace happens—the only question is, will we notice it happening?

IF WE REMEMBER THE PRACTICE
OF CONSCIOUS CONNECTION IT WILL BE
HARD TO MISS.

Some say time is passing too quickly
but is it possible that it is we who are passing
through time too quickly?

Is Your Timepiece "Keeping" You?

> Time is but the stream I go fishing in. I drink at it, but while I drink I see the sandy bottom and detect how shallow it is. Its thin current slides away, but eternity remains.
>
> ~ HENRY DAVID THOREAU

Being an avid student of mindfulness—the practice of being fully present in the moment—the subject of time has always fascinated me because it—or perhaps more accurately stated, our perception of it—affects our lives in ways we seldom consider. Odds are you are wearing a watch right now, or carrying a phone with a digital clock, or sitting in front of a computer with a time display that you have looked at it within the past fifteen minutes. It seems time has us surrounded! Have you given much thought to how much of your life is kept and controlled by "time"? This is not to say we could or should do away with all these wonderful time "keeping" devices because, as someone said, the concept of linear time is what keeps everything from happening all at once. There would be great havoc in our world without a mutual agreement among us about what time it is at any given moment. In other words, we need a way to measure the manner in which life intersects with itself by means of human beings coming and going without chaos ensuing. The question is, can we live mindfully with our various timekeepers rather than being dominated by them?

While Hollywood has made countless entertaining movies about the space-time continuum and time travel, the great irony is that few of us "take time" to consider the phenomenon of time and the role it plays in our daily lives, not to mention the power we give to something we can't even see. What is time? You can't see it, touch it, taste it, smell it, or hear it. Is it, as Thoreau infers, sacred and eternal and at the same time temporal, like a stream that we metaphorically stand in and experience as it passes us by. Does time really even exist or is it simply a creation of human beings seeking to have something tangible by means of which they can measure the duration of their experience on the planet?

The relevancy of time and its impact upon our lives is an ancient conversation.

While I am neither a physicist nor a clock maker, I saw firsthand the work of those who were at the Galileo Museum in Florence, Italy. The museum had on display the inventions of many scientists from the 1600s, and it was apparent that our fascination (and obsession) with the concept of time and space goes back a long way. There were dozens of early timekeeping devices. It got me thinking about the reality that it was human beings who invented time, first by use of a sundial and later by placing numbers on a calendar and then by placing them on a man-made device called a clock. Over the centuries, the position of the sun and stars, calendars, and clocks have aided us in maintaining our lives in a linear fashion based on three "tenses" —past, present, and future—that, pun intended, make us "tense" much of the time.

The Universe knows nothing about time; it is we who created time and live our lives according to the watch strapped to our wrist and the clocks in our home, on the dashboard of our car, or our mobile devices. Suffice it to say, we are prisoners of time, and it seems we can't escape the gravitational pull of its effect on us—or can we? Interestingly enough, a week before being in Florence while presenting at a conference in Geneva, a very kind gentleman named Erik gave me a wristwatch that rather than numbers had the word "Now" at every designated hour. I loved the message! The obvious practice when looking at it is to bring the wearer's mind back into alignment with his body, which is always in the present moment. The fact is, it is always Now; five minutes from now it will still be Now . . . and five years from now it will still be Now—but Now is seldom where our minds are.

My point is this: too often we may hear ourselves saying that time is moving so fast that we can't keep up with it, when in reality, time isn't moving at all. Time is stationary because it is always Now. Perhaps it is we who are moving so quickly through the Now moment we miss the gift of Infinite Presence that is always (and only) available in the present. *Now* is where the grandeur and wonder of life are happening but when our minds are elsewhere we miss the show! It is amazing what one can see when one is completely present in the moment rather than staring at the clock, a time machine that rips us out of the sacred second at hand. If you are open to the idea of reclaiming some of the power you have given to the illusion of time, consider this brief mindfulness practice:

- Using Thoreau’s metaphor, take a few deep breaths and visualize yourself standing comfortably, ankle deep, in a beautiful stream.
- With your feet soundly planted on the sandy bottom, visualize the stream of water rapidly passing over your ankles as “time” flowing by, and the bottom upon which you stand stationary as the present and eternal moment of “Now.”
- For a few minutes breathe deeply and let the water flow with no attachment to where it is going. Just focus on standing firmly, with grace and ease, on the solid sand under your feet. It actually feels good to not get caught up in the current of time doesn’t it?
- Feel a sense of peace slowly rise up within you, from the bottom of your feet . . . up into your heart . . . and then into your head, knowing you have just anchored yourself in the eternal present moment of Now, which is where life is patiently waiting for you to show up.

Sir Noel Coward wrote, “Time is the reef upon which all our frail mystic ships are wrecked.” I think this is a very poetic way of reminding us to be present in the moment where the true Self is always at the helm. When we make space for Infinite Presence to reveal Itself in the present moment, time seems to stand still, allowing us to pilot our mystic vessel more mindfully around the reefs of everyday life. Ram Dass must have had Thoreau in mind when he coined the phrase, "Be here now." This is great advice for us anytime we find ourselves being mesmerized by a clock in its many manifestations. Time really is the reef upon which our mystic ship gets hung up. So take a deep breath right now . . . and enjoy this present moment because, irrespective of what the numbers on your favorite timepiece may say, *Now* is all you really have.

DON'T SQUANDER IT
BY TRYING TO KEEP UP WITH SOMETHING
THAT REALLY DOESN'T EXIST.

Making peace with the fact that we are triune beings is a lifetime practice. Bringing spirit, mind, and body into alignment is a moment-to-moment discipline that changes everything.

The Art of Balancing Your Humanity with Your Divinity

> The teaching of the mystics has been that there should be a conscious courting of the Divine Presence. There should be a conscious receptivity to It, but a balanced one.
>
> ~ ERNEST HOLMES, *THE SCIENCE OF MIND*

As Buddha sat under the Bodhi Tree waiting for enlightenment, two musicians were arguing about the sound they were trying to get from their stringed instrument and distracted him. He was weak and tired from not eating or taking care of his body, but he wanted to see what was causing the commotion and so he dragged himself closer to hear them. One musician would tighten the strings and the other would cry, "Not too tight because you will break the string." The other would counter by saying, "Not too loose because the string will only buzz and rattle—in the middle is just right." The master heard the wisdom contained in their argument and declared, "That's it! That's the key. . . perfect balance! Not too tight yet not too loose, not too high yet not too low, not too in yet not too out. The middle path is the way!"

~ EXCERPT FROM *THE ART OF BEING: 101 WAYS TO PRACTICE PURPOSE IN YOUR LIFE,* DENNIS MERRITT JONES

While this story is ancient in years and only one of various versions of the Buddha's awakening to the premise of the middle pathway, it is nonetheless relevant to our lives today. Finding the appropriate balance between "not too much" and "not too little" is vital to our well-being, health, and happiness, especially when it comes to integrating our Divinity with our humanity. Whether we are talking about the time we dedicate (or don't) to our sacred practices *versus* the time spent (or not) on the necessities of living in the material world, seeking balance between the two is essential for a life of wholeness. Buddha himself had ignored the well-being of his body while trying to achieve enlightenment through the realization of his unity with the All. And, it would appear, by totally detaching from the physical world, he suffered the effects of being out of balance. Regardless of whether we choose to honor it or ignore it, we too are no less affected by the same principle of balance. We must choose wisely how we balance the sacred journey inward with the experiences we encounter on our journey through the human experience.

> Since we cannot contract the Absolute
> we shall have to expand the relative.
>
> ~ DR. ERNEST HOLMES, *THE SCIENCE OF MIND*

I understand that the topic of balancing our humanity with our Divinity is sacred ground for most of us who have dedicated our lives to living in alignment with the awareness that God is All that is. The ability to fully embody and live in the consciousness of First Cause is the Holy Grail that we all seek to embrace and demonstrate every waking moment of our lives. However, while I can't speak for anyone other than myself, at times I admittedly find it challenging to straddle that invisible fence of oneness between the Absolute and the relative.

Living in a physical body automatically puts us into the game of life, which is a full contact sport. The fact is, if we are alive we are in the game whether we like it or not; and we will experience many painful bumps and bruises, some of which may be very difficult to ignore! As diligently as I continue to "court the Presence" (i.e. honor my spiritual aspirations by focusing on sacred practices) there are times when the gravitational pull of the human condition (earth) can suck me out of divine orbit (heaven) rather quickly. I don't believe it is because I lack hours in the sacred saddle, learning and practicing spiritual principles. No doubt, practice does make perfect, but maybe that's the problem. Perhaps at times, some of us have a tendency to misinterpret what the word "perfect" really means when it comes to living as a spiritual being in a human skin. I have seen more than one dedicated student suffer senseless, often self-induced shame because they were not being "spiritual enough" to transcend the conditions with which they were dealing. I believe this is because they had not yet fully integrated their Divinity with their humanity, bringing all the parts together as one whole. To live with spiritual integrity and wholeness is the practice of skillfully blending our spiritual *beingness* with our human *doingness* while never losing sight of either. As Dr. Holmes wrote in *The Science of Mind,* "The only guarantee of our Divinity is in its expression through our humanity."

The art of balancing our humanity with our Divinity rests in our ability to allow for the Presence of the Divine smack dab in the middle of the apparent yuck, muck, and mire of our fully human experience. We do this by knowing that our less than perfect experience is perfectly sacred, nonetheless. I liken this process to be analogous with the idea that we can be "perfectly imperfect" in our humanness. I would like to think that this is what Dr. Holmes had in mind when he stated that our conscious courting of the Divine Presence should be a *balanced one.* A conscious courting of the Presence (which is, without question, Perfect) requires our balancing how we approach living as spiritual beings in a world that sometimes appears less than perfect. The wisdom of "not too *in* yet not too *out*... *in* the middle is just right," somehow seems appropriate.

> We enter the Absolute through that which appears to be finite, because the finite must be drawn from the Infinite.
>
> ~ ERNEST HOLMES, *THE SCIENCE OF MIND*

As spiritually evolving beings expressing life in an expanding universe where everything that *is* originates from one Infinite, Omnipresent, Omnipotent, Omniscient Power, we naturally seek absolute singularity in our oneness with (and as) the Divine. However, like it or not, our existence on this planet is dual in nature; the quintessence of spirit needs the density of material form to express and fulfill its purpose on this planet. Let us be very clear. To say our existence is "dual" in nature does not mean there is duality. Out of, through, from, and as the One, comes the relative—from the One comes the many. This is the juicy irony of earth life itself, and it presents quite a conundrum: In practical application, as spiritual beings having a human experience, it is safe to say that "the Absolute needs the relative and the relative needs the Absolute," and to deny or discount the value, meaning, and purpose of either is not wise. We each need a body in which to "be." The key is to not get *lost* in the body and forget who we *really* are, yet at the same time, to *remember* that while the relative is but a reflection of the Absolute, it is still the *only* way that our heavenly spirit has to touch the earth. This is *why we have come here, is it not?* To touch the earth in ways that give meaning and purpose to life. Here again, the singularity of the One expresses Itself in a multiplicity of form through the dual nature of life: Divinity clothing Itself as humanity. With this understanding, the ancient saying "I am in this world but not of it" more easily finds a home in our minds *and* hearts. Consciously living with our feet on the ground and our mind and heart in the spiritual Ethers of Infinite Intelligence enables us to align and connect our Divinity with our humanity at the same time, and it is a balancing act that affects every area of our lives.

What does it mean to restore our balance?

To "restore" means to bring back to the original condition. Someone once said, "I'm not as close to God as I once was." The only question then is, "Who moved?" Certainly not the God that Is All that Is! At the moment of our physical birth our Divinity was in perfect balance and alignment with our humanity. The more time we've spent on the earth plane, the more influential the lure of the human condition has become—with all of its perceived pleasures, pains, cares, concerns, losses, and gains—all of which tend to give us a strong dose of spiritual amnesia. Balance is defined as "a natural state of equilibrium." The universe (seen and unseen) is in a perpetual state of perfect equilibrium or balance. It is we who, for various reasons, seem to fall out of alignment with this Infinite center point. Therefore, it is up to us to find our way back to the original natural state of equilibrium we knew when first we were born: that moment when our Divine Essence wedded and became one with the complex density of the human body.

If, through the process of conscious self-inquiry,
we discern that our lives could use a bit
of rebalancing by bringing our
humanity into alignment with our Divinity,
where might we start?

The first step in restoring the balance between our humanity and our Divinity is to be conscious enough to know when we are out of balance. Speaking from personal experience, one telltale sign that I am out of balance is when my sleep cycle is off. The more out of balance my sleep cycle, the more difficult it is for me to be focused and present in the moment, which is where my humanity can consciously interface with my Divinity. It's sort of a spiritual quandary. If we are not mindful it is quite easy to take the challenges of the human condition to bed with us, where it will want to wrestle with us all night, pulling us even further out of alignment. How do I restore balance to my sleep cycle? I remember to remember to include an awareness of God's Presence as I close my eyes and silently affirm, "God is" on my in-breath and "I am" on my out-breath. Repeating this mantra I usually quietly drift off within three minutes! And, even if I awaken periodically throughout the night, I come back to this simple practice and am asleep in minutes. The lesson for me is to consciously remember to balance my humanity with my Divinity, even in the quiet of night.

Another place in my life where an imbalance between my humanity and my Divinity occasionally reveals itself is in my relationships. I have noticed that when I am feeling a lack of patience, or I am being a bit grouchy and judgmental, it is because my egoic (human) self has forgotten to include the awareness of God's Presence in that relationship. A remembrance of Infinite Presence brings with it reverence, which then begets words and actions reflecting that reverence. When I remember, balance returns and with it, the ability to truly enjoy the relationship. These are but two examples pulled from the pages of my own life experience. There is no area of our lives where we can't restore balance between our humanity and our Divinity if we are willing to do the work. Would you like to begin to restore the balance between your humanity and your Divinity? Conscious self-inquiry is the first step. Take time to examine the primary areas of your life where you may feel the most out of balance and see where the wisdom of "not too *up* yet not too *down* . . . not too *in* yet not too *out*" might be applied. If you are willing to be completely honest with yourself, you'll know instantly when you are out of balance. The middle pathway is really not difficult to find; it's a matter of staying on it.

A word of caution: At times we may struggle so hard to "court the Presence" that we get in our own way, and in the process we experience an even wider perceived gap between our humanity and our Divinity. When this happens it's important that we don't beat ourselves up with the metaphysical hammer of guilt by saying, "What's in my consciousness to create this experience?" Just get back in the saddle and keep on keeping on. Know that in Truth you can never be closer to the Divine than you are at this moment. Experiencing the Reality of Its Presence, however, happens only when you allow yourself to settle back and make space for the Divine to reveal Itself. Even if you catch only glimpses of It between the cracks and crevices of the experience you are having, have faith—It is there. Just contemplating the ageless question, "Where does my spirit end and my body begin?" will get you thinking about what a sacred experience your life *already* is—warts, wrinkles, and all.

Dr. Holmes was spot on: The only guarantee of your Divinity is in its expression through your humanity. Balancing your humanity with your Divinity is simply living consciously at the hub of your life where your *being* and your *doing* intersect with the presence of God. The effect of such a balancing act will no doubt be your own little slice of Heaven right here on earth, right now.

HOW SWEET IS THAT!

Anger really isn't the problem.
It's about something far more subtle that brews below the surface—resentment.

The Anatomy of **Anger**

Speak when you are angry and you will make the best speech you will ever regret.

~ AMBROSE BIERCE

Over the years I have become an avid student of energy and how it moves. What I have discovered is that as human beings, not only do we consist of pure energy, we are also conduits through which it flows. Once we understand that thought is energy in one of its purest forms we'll become aware that the thoughts we think make us energy directors. Thus, when we have misguided thoughts fueled by the energy of anger our words can be very destructive.

When I was a kid, I had a hair-trigger temper. By the time I was a teen it didn't take much to set me off and ignite my anger. Years later I discovered that I had real issues around my physical stature. Being the skinniest, shortest kid in the schoolyard made me a moving target for the local bullies and just about any of my peers. As an adult I began to understand where my anger was coming from: my own sense of inferiority and defensiveness. On more than one occasion thoughts of anger fueled by enraged emotions sent misguided words soaring out of my mouth that I later regretted. As I matured I discovered that once words are spoken in a moment of misguided passion (rage), they cannot be called back. It's sort of like launching a guided missile and then realizing there is no "abort and destroy" button once it has been launched. Sometimes our misguided words can be like misguided missiles if we are not mindful.

As I began to study Ernest Holmes and the universal law of cause and effect and how the energy of anger moves from cause (thought plus feeling) resulting in effect (words or actions), I came to understand that I play an undeniable role in being the creator of my own experience. This does not mean that I always have control over what others say or do at any given moment, but it does mean I always have absolute control over how I choose to respond to what has been said or done. No doubt, people can say and do some incredibly cruel and thoughtless things that can understandably trigger our anger. However, at the end of the day, without exception, justified or not, it is we who suffer the toxic effects of being the conduit or vessel through which that energy of anger flows.

To be clear, there is really nothing wrong with anger *if* it is expressed in a healthy manner which does no one harm. Anger needs to be identified, understood, ventilated, and released in a manner that is proactive rather than reactive. The operative word in the prior sentence is "released." Why? Buddha wrote, "Holding on to anger is like grasping a hot coal with the intent of throwing it at someone else; you are the one who gets burned." In other words, the misguided missiles of anger we fire at others always come home to roost. It is the acidic energy of long-term resentment that does a slow burn underneath our conscious awareness that does the real damage. Anger "expressed" in a mindless manner is simply an outward sign that the fire of resentment is burning within, below the surface, and needs to be extinguished. The question is, where do we begin the process?

It has been said that
behind all anger is fear in one of its
scariest disguises.

Anger often comes from a deep sense of powerlessness. Consider the idea that all fear arises from a concern of loss. Now, consider the idea that anger is an outward manifestation of an inner fear of loss of power, a loss of control over something or someone, including their behavior. *A Course in Miracles* states, "Anger is a cry for love." When I flash back to my own childhood experiences around anger I can see that my anger was really a cry for love and acceptance based on a belief that somehow I wasn't good enough (lovable) just as I was. Love seems to be the universal antidote for the toxin of anger, once it is understood. Buddha also wrote, "Let a man overcome anger by love." Let us know this applies to little boys and girls as well as adults.

As a mindfulness practice today, consider becoming the observer of your thoughts and feelings, remembering that the presence of the Divine exists at the center of each of us as unconditional Love. It is there and It is accessible—we need only remember to call on It. So perhaps the next time we come across the energy of anger within ourselves or another, we might first consider pausing, taking a deep intentional breath, and before we react and send misguided missiles hurling out of our mouth, silently ask ourselves, "What (or who) needs to be loved here?"

WE MIGHT JUST SAVE OURSELVES FROM
MAKING THE BEST
SPEECH WE'LL EVER REGRET.

Music calls us home.
It reminds us that beyond all the apparent differences
we seem to have, we all come from the same
place—our unity in spirit.

Could Music Help Heal the World?

Music is the universal language,
and love is the key
To peace hope and understanding,
and living in harmony . . .

~ MAC DAVIS

When Mac Davis penned these lyrics for his 1970s classic pop song, "I Believe in Music," he was expressing what just about every musician of the time was feeling when he sang or played an instrument. It certainly was true for me, and I suspect for anyone who has ever been a musician, and shall be as long as music moves through the hearts and souls of human beings. The spoken and unspoken sentiment most every musician and music lover will attest to is that music holds the power to unify human beings.

The spiritual significance of music is that it brings people together at a level of vibration that transcends boundaries, culture, language, religion, gender, age, color, and politics —a place where we can all experience our sameness. When we can move beyond all labels, our differences tend to dissolve into the oneness from which we came. How can the energy of music be this powerful? Music resonates with the heart, not just the head.

While there is indeed a mathematical element to music that requires the integration of the left brain with the right brain, when music flows it penetrates and permeates the heart and soul of every human being it touches. For most of us, music is not an intellectual process; it is an emotional experience that is uniquely personal and yet at the same time, interpersonal—it's what connects us with others. While we may need an interpreter to tell us what the lyrics of a song mean, no one needs an interpreter to tell us what the energy of music is saying—the heart knows. In the words of my singer-songwriter friend Harold Payne, "Music speaks louder than words, it's the only thing that the whole world listens to."

From the day when humankind first discovered music by beating a stick on a hollow log, to this moment in time, the music that flows through us is really the outer manifestation of an inner urge to express life. The word *express* means to press out. When music erupts from within us it is the desire of the soul seeking to push out and "be." When music becomes a shared experience with others, it is simply the soul seeking to push out and spill over into the souls of others in a creative process where their energies blend in amazing ways.

As musicians, when we commingle our desire to express through our music, and we experience it together, we create something that no one of us could create alone. When this happens, it is literally divine harmony as the soul rejoices in its oneness with something far greater than the individual "I." Some of my most intense and blissful peak moment experiences have happened while playing music with others.

Music calls us home. It reminds us that beyond all the apparent differences we seem to have, we all come from the same place—our unity in spirit. That is the power and significance of music. Whether you create music or just enjoy listening to it, music brings us together to celebrate, co-create and express the joy we find in our oneness, while at the same time honoring how it is expressed through us as individuals in such unique and creative ways. So the next time you turn on your TV, radio, or iPod, or go to a movie or a concert, pay attention to the music and imagine what your world might be like without it. Then, thank a musician for being the instrument through which it all flows.

Could music *really* help heal the world of its many problems? What I know is this: When we are conscious enough to consider it, music is simply that which invites us to "remember to remember" that we are never separate or alone, and that we have far more in common with our earth family than we have differences. And when we remember that connection, we all have a tendency to treat one another with more loving kindness, generosity, compassion, and respect. If music can open the door to humankind's heart to a point where we really do see ourselves in one another, anything is possible. I agree with

Harold Payne—music really does speak louder than words, and it's a language we can all speak. So turn up your CD player and sing along! Let the world know that you believe in music—it might just catch on.

AND IN THE PROCESS
BRING THE PEOPLE ON THIS PLANET
CLOSER TOGETHER.

It's never too late
to reawaken the explorer within
and venture where we have never been before.

Expand Your Vision of a Life Worth Living

> Man's experience is the logical outcome of his inner vision; his horizon is limited to the confines of his own consciousness. Whenever this consciousness lacks a true perspective, its outward expression will lack proper harmony.
>
> ~ ERNEST HOLMES

For thousands of years, explorers and adventurers have faithfully gazed to the stars above and the horizon below—that pristine place where the sky and earth appear to come together—as a point to mark their path before making the journey to places yet unseen. They understood that if they wanted to expand their horizon they had to leave the convenience of their current location and lean into the mystery of the unknown that lay before them—beyond what the human eye could perceive. Whether by foot, horseback, wagon train, ship, airplane, or now, spacecraft, the horizon has long wooed us to come closer and see what we have not seen before; to experience a greater dimension of a life worth living and, in the process, find meaning and purpose in the journey.

Irrespective of our age, there lies within each of us an explorer who yearns for higher ground, a vantage point from which to garner an expanded view of life and the boundless possibilities that come with thinking outside the box of the known. When we were young, that explorer within was continually seeking new territory (just look at any toddler for proof of this theory), but over the years the spirit of the inner explorer became very domesticated, being taught for "our own good" never to venture too far outside the safety zone of the known. And there, in a very comfortable box, many of us have set up camp . . . perhaps curious about the mysteries and wonders that new horizons hold for us but never moving toward them to make the discovery for ourselves. The good news is, it's never too late to reawaken that explorer within and expand our horizons! The quintessential question is, how do we make that leap . . . what is the first step? The answer may lie in reigniting the sense of awe and wonder we had about the Universe when we were young.

When did you last take the time to gaze upward on a clear night and scan the infinite canopy of stars, contemplating where the edge of the Universe might be, and perhaps wondering what your role is in the grand scheme of such an amazing cosmic story spanning fourteen billion years? If it has been a while, you may want to consider some stargazing one night soon—it will energize you and awaken that explorer spirit within. I remember star-gazing as a young boy and I still make a practice of doing so from time to time. I never seem to tire when it comes to pondering the immensity, complexity, and unity of a Universe continually pushing out, expanding at 186,282 miles per second. To merely entertain this fact boggles my mind while at the same time, it compels me to continue the quest to understand and actualize my unique role in the cosmos.

When I was ten years old I didn't intellectually comprehend the spiritual significance, let alone the miracle, of the Universe and all that is contained within it, but even then I innately sensed that I belonged. I knew that I was part of something expansive . . . something far greater than myself that had an intelligent, structured pattern of orderliness that seemed to know what it was doing. Surely, if this intelligence knew how to hold the stars and planets in place for countless millennia—while, at the same time, expanding at the speed of light—it would know how to hold my life in place through all of fifth grade and perhaps well beyond, even over the distant horizon called sixth grade. Thinking back, this awareness alone gave me a feeling of inner peace which engendered a sense of confidence that my life and presence on the planet wasn't the byproduct of some causal, accidental, cosmic explosion, but that I was meant to be here and that my life had purpose and meaning yet to be discovered.

The explorer spirit in you knows this is true about you as well. Can you relate? I invite you to consider this question intently because how you answer it will determine how you interpret your *relationship* with Life. Because the Universe is expanding exponentially at the speed of light, your perspective of the Universe and therefore, your relationship *with* the Universe, is essential. You will feel either minuscule, insignificant, separate, and apart *from* it all or—just the opposite—a great and vital part *of* it all. Explorers inherently know they are an intricate part of a grand Universe; they sense the sacred spark, the burning ember within, that affirms they are one with the expanding Light from which they came.

> The cosmos is within us.
> We are made of star-stuff.
> We are a way for the universe to know itself.
>
> ~ CARL SAGAN

As astronomer Carl Sagan points out, you are an individuated expression of an Infinite Universe seeking to know Itself finitely. Imagine that! In other words, not only are you part of something far greater than yourself, (regardless of whether you know it, or like it, or not), you also have a role to play—and that is to be a unique microcosm of the grand macrocosm, a self-knowing, living, expanding Universe. This means all the attributes of the macrocosm must *already* exist within the microcosm. The only question is, shall you fulfill that role consciously or by default, unconsciously? The explorer in you knows that the more conscious you are in your quest, the more power you will actualize from within. To realize you are a *conscious* conduit through which the Universe is expanding is profoundly empowering; it means you have become an intentional co-creator with *the* Creator and, therefore, new horizons are not only possible, they are compellingly reachable.

Honoring the Divine Urge Is the Fast Track to New Horizons

> If we want truly extraordinary vision then you have to continually expand your horizons, take risks. If we don't push our edge we'll never expand our view. It's not trespassing to go beyond your own boundaries.
>
> ~ DEWITT JONES

The first principle of a living Universe is expansion; this means there is an impulse within each of us that is constantly pushing out (the explorer's spirit), seeking to express and know more of itself *through us* in new ways. Ernest Holmes referred to this impulse as the "Divine Urge." When we sense this divine nudge trying to gain our attention and we choose to give way to it, it lifts us (in consciousness) to see new horizons, new possibilities we never before knew existed. One definition for the word *horizon* is, "the limit of a person's mental perception, experience, or interest." The operative word in this definition is "limit"; our perceived horizon sets the limit on our view of life—we can see no further than the horizon. So the question is, do we try to "expand" the horizon itself, <u>or our view of the horizon</u>?

Anyone who has ever flown in an airplane knows the higher you ascend, the more expansive the horizon is and thus, the greater your perspective becomes. Nothing "out there" necessarily changes, but how you see it changes immensely. This is not just a metaphor; it's how consciousness works; it determines the horizon to which we can/will aspire. Since your life experience always rises to the rim of your consciousness (or belief system)—and no higher—and finds expression at that level, by establishing a conscious awareness of your oneness with the Universe you'll be more likely to find your place in the Universe . . . and, conversely—and equally important—you'll be able to find *its* place in you.

Arriving at this point of awareness is important because it is the fulcrum at which you *consciously* merge with the Infinite where life truly becomes a sacred journey. As Emerson inferred, this is when you can "hitch your wagon to a star." As you align with and ride the cosmic wave of expansion that inherently pulsates in and through all living things, you are lifted to a new perspective and as a result, a new "horizon of reality" appears before you. As you rise in consciousness you begin to see things differently—as from an elevated plane—through the eyes of an explorer.

This does not mean you live in the fifth-dimensional ethers of some alternate reality. At birth you were given an earth suit (body) in which to circumnavigate *this* planet, so you belong here with your feet firmly planted on terra firma. Your role here is to be a conscious conduit by means of which the Infinite knows itself as the finite—this is where and how heaven touches earth, through and by means of you. This is also what awakens the explorer's spirit within. With this heightened perspective you are free to explore and move through the human condition with an enhanced purview of Life, knowing you are able to seek and find new expanded horizons *right before your eyes,* between the in-and-outs and the ups-and-downs of your daily life. You don't require cosmic enlightenment to expand your consciousness or your horizon—just an awareness of your oneness with Life and an understanding of how an expanding Universe conspires to enlarge upon itself in and through you every moment of every day.

There is a larger life waiting for us just beyond our current reality. The Infinite One is continually offering us an expanded vision of life wherein all things are possible, but we must first have eyes to see it and the courage to pursue it. It may require examining our current belief system, and if necessary, challenging what we find lingering therein that may be holding us back. To transcend the boundaries that we (or others) have previously set is a high calling—but the reward for those who stay the course is immense. When we establish and embrace an inner vision of the life we wish to live and then faithfully follow where it leads, new opportunities will open before us like clouds in the sky parting on a windy day. Whoever said, "The sky is the limit" must not have realized that it's not the sky that limits us—it's our perception of the sky that determines the span of the horizon that calls us to new levels of self-expression and fulfillment.

The quintessential question is, what new horizon is calling you today? Has it caught your attention? It's there if you are willing to open your eyes and look up! Can you SEE far enough to catch the vision of the life that lingers, waiting for you just beyond that horizon? The bigger question is, can you hold your eye on that vision and continue toward it through fair weather or foul, good times or bad? Even if you are uncertain that you can make the journey—not to worry; your inner explorer knows the way and is ready to depart when you are. Taking action is a prerequisite. It's one thing to stand and stare at the horizon from a safe distance and quite another to move toward it. The wonderful thing is, upon your arrival at your destination, if you pause and gaze into the distance, you will discover additional new horizons beckoning you . . . inviting you to come closer and explore the next "that which is yet to be." Therein lies the beauty and meaning to be found in pursuing new horizons; they remind us that, because we live in an expanding Universe, there is more for us to know and more for us to grow, and—as long as we live on this beautiful planet—there always will be. If you would expand your vision of a life worth living, the first thing to remember is, the sky is *not* the limit—only your perception of the sky can limit you—and the explorer within knows it.

ARE YOU READY TO GO?

Seek to truly understand the power of your word. With it you can heal or hurt, build up or beat down the people you love and care about.

Being Impeccable in Our Word

> Be impeccable with your word. Speak with integrity. Say only what you mean. Avoid using the word to speak against yourself or to gossip about others. Use the power of your word in the direction of truth and love.
>
> ~ DON MIGUEL RUIZ, *THE FOUR AGREEMENTS*

While sitting in a restaurant I had a major league "ah-ha" that really whacked me upside the head, and I would like to share this realization with you. Perhaps you might be able to relate with it (or at least know someone who will ☺) because at first glance it appears to be a very innocuous form of behavior based on the fact that we all tend to do it on a regular basis. It seems to be inculcated in our culture. Perhaps for that very reason it is something we all need to pay attention to because it affects the emotional (and thus physical) well-being of all of us. The "it" to which I am referring is gossip and the mindless spreading of hearsay, comments, and rumors.

As I sat trying to mind my own business while eating my lunch, the people in the booth directly behind me were having someone by the name of Jane for lunch . . . and she wasn't even there! I honestly did my best to dial it out but the energy of their conversation was all-pervasive. They were "consuming" her character, talking about her in such a disparaging manner that it was painful to hear. It was in that moment that I became aware that I have also on occasion been a target of the same sort of mindless, groundless gossip and rumors, and yes, I too, have also feasted on savory gossip and noshed on tasty unfounded rumors with others. In a microsecond, I understood that the pain I was feeling for Jane and those who were talking about her had became my pain because they were a reflection of me.

At some point or another in our lives we have all been the target of gossip and rumors, as well as participants in the spreading of them. It is insidious, toxic, and yet, oh so juicy. Unless we are mindful and vigilant, it's quite easy to fool ourselves into believing that what is coming from our minds, mouths, and hearts is harmless idle chatter. That's how gossip works. It's hard to detect when we are in the process of gossiping because it is provocative and seductive, but most of all, it is destructive.

Why is it that gossip is so prevalent among us?

Many people find some sort of power in gossip because it represents "inside" knowledge that not everyone else is privy to. Some people find great comfort in knowing they can commiserate (share their misery) with like-minded people, while others may find gossip and the spreading of rumors a passive/aggressive way of dealing with their feelings of jealousy or envy, or perhaps their own insecurities and fears. Still, for others, it may mean that by putting someone else down (who is seldom present) it somehow makes themselves feel more important. The reasons we gossip are legion: however, not one of them justifies the activity.

This message is a reminder of how easy it is to jump into the stagnate pool of mindless gossip in our workplace, our church, the doctor's office, the grocery store, and even our own homes and neighborhoods. From a spiritual perspective, understanding we are all one, it means that when we gossip to others about others we are ultimately doing damage to ourselves as well. Beyond the spiritual reality is the fact that any person who will gossip *with you* about others will also gossip *about you* with others. I guess it's an instant karma sort of thing. Any way you cut it, gossip and the spreading of rumors are counterproductive to creating a healthy relationship with life. Speaking with integrity in our daily interactions is a conscious choice we get to make every day.

Take the Test

I invite you to join me in using this test before we unleash words that may be less than impeccable. Before speaking to or about another person, mindfully ask yourself these questions:

1. Is what I am about to say true? Do I know beyond a shadow of a doubt that what I am repeating is accurate and true, or is

it based on hearsay and assumptions that I or others have made without gathering all the facts from an impartial and reliable source?

2. What will I gain from repeating these words to others? Will what I am going to say be life affirming, productive, and helpful to all involved and will the world be a better place because I uttered these words? If not, why would I want to repeat them?

3. Is what I am about to say about another person something I would have the clarity, courage, and commitment to say to his face, and if so, why don't I do so?

4. Will what I am going to say be using the power of my word in the direction of truth and love?

Before we speak, or hit the forward and send button, it would do us well to pause and become witness to our thoughts before they become our words. I invite you to join me in using the power of your word in an intentional and conscious manner. Not just because speaking with integrity is the right thing to do, but because the world needs and deserves the absolute highest and best that we can bring to it.

When we gossip and spread rumors—when we speak less than impeccably about others—we are affirming to the universe that hears our every word that we feel separate and apart from the whole of life. We are declaring *our own* lack of wholeness. When we are not impeccable in our word we participate in creating pain and suffering for others, and that is not why we have come to earth. When we use our word in the direction of truth and love, we honor God's presence by creating harmony and peace, and *that* is why we are here.

What we think and say matters, so being impeccable with our word seems like a great place to start.

NOW, <u>THAT</u> IS WORTH REPEATING,
SO PASS IT ON!

Life is not designed to be lived in a straight line. Moving up, down, and sideways is part of the ride—and keeping your balance is the practice of a lifetime.

A Life Worth Living Doesn't Follow a Straight Line

> Progress has not followed a straight ascending line, but a spiral with rhythms of progress and retrogression, of evolution and dissolution.
>
> ~ GOETHE

As Goethe inferred, life is not a straight ascending ride but more like a universal roller coaster—an endless continuum of dips, rises, and spirals; of beginnings and endings . . . successes and failures . . . wins and losses . . . setbacks and advances . . . good days and bad days . . . peaks and valleys . . . light and darkness. In the human realm we can't have one without the other because we need the contrast of one to give meaning to the other. We just need to remember that this is so and to keep moving, whether we are on an "ascending or a bending" part of the ride. Life is rife with changes and challenges that perpetually come and go. Throughout the ages masters have described this universal principle as the "heartthrob" of Life, always pulsating in a circular manner that serves the creation, evolution, and, ultimately, the dissolution of all living things. What matters is our perspective of the process and understanding as to how it affects every area of our lives. The ancient wise ones have reminded us that all that "is" has a beginning and an end, where there is a period of rest (or restoration) between what was and what shall be. But they never described that period as a permanent stopping place. Just as the planets have cycles, our lives have cycles: day ends with night, night with day; summer ends with fall, fall with winter, and on it goes. In short, life is one wild ride on a universal spiral. The secret of the ages has been to experience the ride, the beginnings and the endings, the good and the bad, and not get consumed by either the positive aspects or the negative. But how do we do this in a world where there appears to be so much chaos that pummels our senses and pulls us in every direction? The practice is called "The Wisdom of Equanimity."

> Even a happy life cannot be without a measure of darkness, and the word happy would lose its meaning if it were not balanced by sadness. It is far better to take things as they come along with patience and equanimity.
>
> ~ CARL JUNG

Equanimity is defined as "mental or emotional calmness or equilibrium." In the context of this writing, equanimity allows us to stand where we are on the ride of life and simply "be" with it. In other words, equanimity is detached observation; it is the practice of being mindfully aware whether we are leaning toward "whatever is" and favoring it, or, pulling away from "whatever is" and disfavoring it and then finding the balance of a neutral position that favors neither. The wisdom of equanimity can be applied when navigating our way through difficult times as well as when dealing with difficult people. It is a mindfulness practice that helps us be the observer of our thoughts and feelings before we act on them in a manner that we may later regret. In Buddhism equanimity might be considered an aspect of walking the middle path because it creates the perfect emotional balance required to stay on the ride and not be seduced by the polarity of life in the human condition.

To cling to the belief that our life is supposed to continually progress in an ascending straight line causes much suffering. If today is a day of curves and bends rather than an ascending straight line, darkness rather than light, sadness rather than happiness, failure rather than achievement, remember that it must have an end just as it had a beginning. Equally important, remember that while it is not to be perceived as permanent, just as a roller coaster stops between rides, there is a period of rest in between the two. Take a breath and fully "be" in that sacred space.

The wisdom of equanimity brings balance to our perspective; it allows us to breathe and experience the sacred gap—the space of what is—that lies between what was and what shall be, knowing as surely as night follows day, this too shall pass.

Remember, there will always be more peaks and valleys ahead on the spiral of life. This is truly great news because it means we're alive . . . and that's a ride worth staying on.

JUST REMEMBER TO BREATHE AND
KEEP YOUR BALANCE!

The world needs more kindness,
but with whom and where does it begin?

The Art of **Being Kind**

So many gods, so many creeds,
So many paths that wind and wind,
While just the art of being kind
Is all the sad world needs.

~ ELLA WHEELER WILCOX

I have been witnessing in my own life how powerful an act of kindness can be and how much fun it can be. I take my garbage cans out to the curb every Sunday night because the trash collectors come early on Monday morning. But for the past few months when I've gone to put the cans back, they are not there. Someone has mysteriously and very stealthily moved them back by the side of the house where they are stored. Now I have heard about people in the drive-through line paying for someone else's coffee at Starbucks, or the fare at a tollbooth, but never have I heard of acts of "trash can" kindness! I suspect it is one of my neighbors, and I must admit it's really got my attention. What his or her motivation is I don't know, but I am interpreting it as a generous and selfless act of kindness. There is something very empowering about extending kindness to others, especially when it can be done anonymously.

This simple act of kindness has me thinking a lot lately about how we as human beings coexist together, not just as neighbors, but as passengers on this ever-shrinking "spaceship earth" as referred to by Buckminster Fuller. Our differences are so vast in so many ways. Between cultural values and traditions, nationalities, religions, politics, and so on, we can feel very isolated at times. Kindness, which I also think of as generosity of spirit, can be the bridge that connects us because it is something to which every human being on the planet can relate. An act of kindness is easily understood and can supersede any language, religious, or cultural gap. In that regard, kindness can be thought of as a universal language we *all* can speak—with our *actions*.

The ancient philosopher Philo of Alexandria (20 BC–50 AD) said, "Be kind, for everyone you meet is fighting a hard battle." It seems some things in the human realm never change, and the normal tendency in tough times may be to withdraw from others because we are so consumed by our own fears, concerns, and problems. However when we withdraw, that's when a sense of isolation comes flooding in. And yet if we think about it, a simple act of kindness to another can instantly reconnect him (and us) to life in ways we may never know. Just think about that. *Your* act could be the bridge that another person needs at that moment to get him or her through the day. And irrespective of how simple you may think it is, there's no such thing as a small act of kindness. Every act of kindness creates a ripple effect that reaches out far beyond that of your own. That's the empowering thing about generosity of spirit—

when we receive kindness we are naturally inspired to extend it to others.

Perhaps Ella Wheeler Wilcox was right—the world needs more kindness, but with whom and where does it begin? Perhaps by being kind you might just be the one to change the world. It could be while standing in line at the grocery store by inviting the person behind you to go ahead of you. It might be by holding a door open for someone. It could be as simple as a welcoming smile . . . or, if you really want to see your neighbor go a bit batty, try the stealth "trash can kindness" maneuver. ☺

Any way you slice it, a deeper experience of kindness is what we all inherently desire. We are hardwired for kindness because it is in our spiritual DNA to treat one another with reverence—with an authentic generosity of spirit. We just have to be mindful of the spiritual beings we really are and the acts of kindness will follow naturally with grace and ease, not because we should be kind, but because we can. To this end I close with one of my favorite quotes by the Dalai Lama: "This is my simple religion. There is no need for temples; no need for complicated philosophy. Our own brain, our own heart is our temple; the philosophy is kindness."

I RATHER LIKE THAT PHILOSOPHY.
HOW ABOUT YOU?

What if we were to spiritualize the practice of "paying attention" by seeing it as an invitation from the Universe to actualize our Wholeness, our Oneness with It?

The Power of Paying Attention

A 3-Step Mindfulness Practice That Will Change How You Experience Life

If we would come to the Universal Wholeness, we must accept it through the law of its own nature. This means that we must give our undivided attention to the spiritual unit back of all things.

~ DR. ERNEST HOLMES

As a child, were you ever repeatedly told to pay attention? I certainly was. Like most kids, I had a very short attention span. Regardless of what I was doing, dialing in on the task at hand seemed to be a major challenge. My mind did an ample amount of wandering in the wonder, focusing on just about anything other than the current moment and what I was supposed to be doing. Can you relate? Even as adults, for many of us paying attention is challenging. It's probably not an exaggeration to say that, irrespective of our age, we still occasionally need a gentle and timely reminder to be present in the moment —and for good reason. As evidence, while casually strolling along the busy sidewalk on my first trip to London, I was surprised at nearly every street crossing to look down and see painted in very large letters the words, LOOK RIGHT. It became instantly clear that looking to the right before stepping off the curb was a wise practice in the UK because that is the direction from which the cars and buses (really big buses) come roaring by. Living in the US, where people drive on the "right" side of the road, I was accustomed to looking to the left for oncoming traffic. I had an instant flashback to my childhood and the mantra that many of our parents gave us at an early age: "Always stop . . . look . . . and listen before crossing the street." I was grateful for the warning signs painted on the sidewalk; they were propitious and timely reminders to pay attention to the moment and what I was doing because if I didn't, there could be dire consequences. Taking that intentional pause was literally a lifesaver.

As children, little did we know it then, but the admonition to "stop, look, and listen" may have been our first introduction to the ancient practice of mindfulness, which according to author Jon Kabat-Zinn means "Paying attention in a particular way, on purpose, in the present moment nonjudgmentally." While mindfulness has been practiced as a discipline in various spiritual teachings for millennia, it is only in the past few years that it has become more mainstream in the corporate and medical world. Why? Because it increases one's ability to pay attention to the moment at hand in a manner that lowers stress levels, which in turn, serves to increase one's productivity in the workplace, and healing and sustained well-being in the patient. It's quite amazing how often our mind splinters itself and habitually rides off in multiple directions at the same time, failing to pay attention to what's happening in the present moment. In the process it's quite easy to get broadsided by something we don't see coming.

The Wisdom of Stop, Look, and Listen Is Universally Applicable

For many of us, over the years the practice of mindfully stopping, looking, and listening has subtlety faded into the recesses of our habit mind only to be unconsciously resurrected through "survival mode" with something like crossing the street. The good news is the conscious practice of taking time to mindfully stop, look, and listen is something that can be integrated into every area of our lives—and it will not only help us survive, but thrive far beyond what we may currently think is possible. As an example, when we approach a crosswalk on a busy intersection, we most likely stop, look, and listen before we step into the street. However, when confronted with a perplexing problem or sudden emergency, do we likewise take time to intentionally stop, look, and listen before we act or react? When we have a difficult choice or decision to make, do we stop, look, and listen before we choose? When we are in a conversation with others, do we stop, look, and listen before we speak?

When we receive a diagnosis or prognosis from our doctor, do we stop, look, and listen before buying into it? When we are challenged by another person's criticism or opinion of us, do we stop, look, and listen before we react? When we lie down to sleep at night, do we stop, look, and listen before we drift off? Clearly the list could go on.

> Perhaps the deeper question is, when we initiate the mindfulness practice of "Stop, Look, and Listen" what are we stopping for —what are we looking for—and what are we listening for?

As we spiritualize the above question, the answer becomes obvious and delightfully simple: God's presence; we are "paying attention" in a particular way, purposefully in the present moment, nonjudgmentally, to experience the presence of the One. We are creating an intentional sacred gap—a moment in time and space—to realize our oneness with God's Omnipresence (Presence), Omnipotence (Power), and Omniscience (Intelligence or All Knowing). It's a matter of training our mind to pay attention to the moment regardless of where we are or what we are doing. As Ernest Holmes wrote in *The Science of Mind,* "Since Spirit is present in Its entirety at all times and in all places it follows that all of Spirit is wherever we center our attention." This awareness assures us that in each moment of paying "nonjudgmental" (i.e., looking beyond conditions) attention to our oneness with Spirit we are accessing whatever we need, not just to survive in the moment but to thrive in the All-ness that is God.

Be it in the form of guidance, wisdom, strength, acceptance, safekeeping, or inner peace; with mindfulness Spirit is, as St. Paul inferred, closer to us than our very breath. Whether we are crossing the street, preparing to sign a business contract, taking a test in school, contemplating what or what not to put into our bodies, facing a life-changing challenge or making a life-changing choice, taking the time to mindfully stop, look, and listen is a wise thing to do. Why? Because it makes space for Infinite Presence to be remembered, revealed, and actualized in whatever form It needs to bring us into alignment with the Whole in that moment. The practice is not difficult once we master the following three-step process. Notice how elegantly simple it is if we take it one step at a time, slowly and mindfully:

1

STOP your body and your mind and take several deep breaths.

There is a natural connection between our head and heart, and that is our breath. We can stop our mind from racing about "willy-nilly" as Ernest Holmes referred to it, by physically stopping our body, taking a few intentionally deep breaths and releasing them very slowly while focusing on our breath and nothing else. Adding a simple silent mantra, such as "God is" on the in-breath and "I am" on the out-breath, will help us slow down and be present in the Presence. Stopping to anchor ourselves in the ground of our Being comes first with our breath being the grounding conduit. Stopping our body, stopping our mind, and paying attention to the moment sets the stage for what is next.

2

LOOK within and realize all that you are
is the Essence of the Divine.

Intentionally withdrawing our gaze from the outer reality to our inner Reality is not always easy because the outer world is so seductive; there is so much going on that we think we need to be part of to survive on the surface of life. As we mindfully begin to look within we descend to the center of our being where we'll discover that sacred part of ourselves that knows that while we may be "in this world" we are not "of this world." Looking within first, rather than to the world, to understand and respond to "what is" in the moment, is the act of a true master. A master is one who knows that "as within, so without" is far more than a catch phrase—it's a way of being—a way of walking a sacred path on the surface of life regardless of where we are or what we are doing.

3

LISTEN to the serene voice of the
Beloved in the silence beneath the chattering mind.

There is a profound difference between hearing and listening. Hearing is a function of the human ear and listening is a function of an attuned, receptive mind and an open heart. Deep listening happens not only with our inner ear but also by means of our emotions and feeling nature. At the deepest level of our being, the voice of the Infinite One communicates by means of our intuition, which is first experienced as a feeling in our heart center which then rises to our mind as an inner knowing. When we are still enough to listen to the serene voice of the Beloved we shall access the wisdom and guidance we seek, experience the well-being that is inherent, and actualize the authentic power that has always been there awaiting our arrival and acceptance.

At the end of the day, the practice of mindfully going to the center of our being by taking time to stop, look, and listen will help us survive our frenzied mind as it zooms across the surface of our daily life, too often forgetting that *it* best serves *us* when it is mindfully anchored in our body. Paying attention to the moment and what we are doing in it isn't really that difficult, especially when we can remember that—in truth—the present moment is all we ever really have. Given this perspective it makes good sense to embrace the gift Life is offering us in this and every precious moment and honor it—the good, the bad and the ugly. Mindfulness is a way to align with Life Itself and never take a moment of it for granted. Perhaps the innate call to pay attention really is an invitation—a divine, albeit subtle, nudge—from the Universe to actualize our Oneness with It. Have you yet accepted the invitation?

JUST STOP, LOOK, AND LISTEN,
AND YOU'LL KNOW.

The "C" word sends a chill down many spines. The "C" word I am referring to is Commitment and it takes you beyond the point of no return.

The Secret to Going the Distance Is Really No Secret

The pathway to the top of the mountain is lined with campsites along the way, occupied by those who yielded to the resistance of walking the path of uncertainty and who weren't able to embody the deeper meaning of commitment to going the distance.

~ EXCERPT FROM *THE ART OF UNCERTAINTY - HOW TO LIVE IN THE MYSTERY OF LIFE AND LOVE IT*

If the fruition of your vision of a life worth living awaited you at the top of a mountain, would you have the commitment to traverse the unknown elements between here and there and go the distance? The metaphorical mountaintop experience we seek can be different for us all: It could be the completion of a college education, or the realization of the career we have long desired. It might be honoring a diet or exercise program long enough to see the results we desire manifest. It could be learning how best to just get through another day by managing a debilitating emotional or physical problem in a manner that allows us to stay connected to a life of purpose and meaning.

For many of us, the mountaintop for which we dream and strive is a deeply rewarding relationship with a lifetime partner. It doesn't much matter what mountain peak we seek because the power of commitment is equally applicable (and available) to every area of our lives—and it is the power that will get us to the top.

Over the span of my adult life there have been numerous occasions when I found myself "waffling in the wind" on some commitment I was about to make, or perhaps had already made, and I needed a "sign" to assure me I could do the right thing and go the distance. Sometimes we need a hero or two who have demonstrated the power of commitment in their own lives to show us the way up the mountain. My heroes were my parents, Russ and Evelyn Jones. Up until almost the time they both passed at ninety-five years young, Mom and Dad were still like a couple of Energizer bunny rabbits . . . and had been able to celebrate their seventy-fifth wedding anniversary together a few months prior. Anyway you slice it, creating and sharing a life together for over seventy-five years is a tremendous example of commitment to an idea that was larger than either of them as individuals. I happen to know firsthand that although they stumbled more than a few times on the many pathways of uncertainty we traveled as a family, they always found the courage, wisdom, and strength to pick themselves up and continue their journey up the mountain with four wild children in tow. That's what the power of commitment does; it is bigger than our obstacles and it sees us through our uncertainties and the temptations to stop short and pitch a tent before we reach the top of our personal mountains—it's what keeps us keeping on long after others have pulled off the path and set up camp in the foothills of unfulfilled dreams.

By example, what I learned from Mom and Dad is that regardless of what your personal mountain may be, and wherever you may be on the pathway at this moment, there is something within you that knows how to get you to the top if you do your part. What is your part, you might ask.

- FIRST, enter each day with faith and an awareness of your oneness with a higher power that is larger than yourself—call it God, the Buddha Nature, the Christ, Life, Infinite Intelligence, the Universe, or whichever word has meaning to you.
- SECOND, approach your chosen pathway with a persistency that has no off switch (like the Energizer Bunny).
- THIRD, to echo the words of author Steven Covey, you must "begin with the end in mind": persevere in holding a vision in your mind's eye that gives purpose and meaning to your life by seeing yourself standing on the mountaintop.
- LASTLY, connect with the passion for life that lives in your heart. Passion is the energy that will bring you to the edge of all you know—it becomes the bridge that spans the gap between where you are on the pathway and where you want to be.

When combined, these four things comprise the essence and power of commitment that will take you where you may have never gone before. What I know is this: Irrespective of the personal mountain you might be climbing, the view of your life from the top is unparalleled. You can take a gentle gaze back and see down the pathway from whence you have come with the pride and satisfaction of knowing that you stayed the course . . . you went the distance. These mountaintop moments are among the sweetest experiences you shall ever have in your life, and they are the moments most worth pursuing. Commitment is, and always has been, the secret to going the distance; it's a choice we get to make daily. Commitment is a prerequisite in creating a life worth living, and it's a power that is no further from you than your next thought, and then the next thought, and then the next thought, followed, of course, by a corresponding action. Begin with the end in mind, indeed . . .

BUT MOST IMPORTANTLY,
JUST BEGIN.

Exactly, what is a world that works for everyone?
Is it really possible . . . does it already exist . . .
what conclusion have you arrived at
in your mind and heart?

A World That Works FOR Everyone Works THROUGH Everyone

> Personal transformation is the first step in global transformation—in creating a world that works for everyone . . . This is the work you can do. Hopefully this will shift one's attention from changing the world to changing himself or herself. I don't know another way to change the world.
>
> ~ GARY ZUKAV, *THE SEAT OF THE SOUL*

It has been called everything from an absolute necessity for humankind's survival to excessively idealistic, totally unrealistic, completely unreachable, pie-in-the-sky thinking. Conversely, it has also been called a nonissue because we already live in a world that works for everyone, and therefore, unnecessary to focus upon. Where individuality is freely expressed there are ample and diverse opinions surrounding the subject of *"a world that works for everyone."* What is yours? Perhaps the word *works* needs to be explored and defined. Does *work* mean to labor, or is it the effort to produce something tangible or of value? Does it mean to the degree something functions well or not well? Perhaps *works* is a euphemism that means agreement or acceptance, as in "That works for me because it serves *my personal* purpose and needs."

As an experiment, I did a little research project to see where people were in their personal beliefs about a world that works for everyone. I began asking friends as well as strangers, these questions: Do you believe a world that works for everyone is possible, and if so, what would have to happen to create such a world? Or do you believe it already exists? The responses I received were vastly diverse; they ranged from profound to perverse.

The world works fine just the way it is—
it's people that are the problem.

In a world that works for everyone, no one would be deprived
of clean water and adequate food and shelter.

In a world that works for everyone we must learn to live
and let live. In other words, leave me alone to make my own way
in the world and I will leave you alone.

Only when there is peace throughout the entire
world will it work for everyone.

Just eliminate all religions—then the world will work for everyone.

Do away with all the labels and judgments we place on
each other that divide us and the world.

When every human being is treated with equality
the world will work for everyone.

We need to kill all people who teach hate if we want
a world that works for everyone.
(Yes, this was a real response to the question.)

The world works just fine for me; it owes me nothing but the freedom to create a life of my own making.

Redistribute the wealth of the world equally among every human being and the world will work for everyone.

The world will never work for everyone because of corporate greed and politicians who serve only their own interest.

The world already works for everyone according to their own beliefs.

Exactly, what *is* a world that works for everyone, and where might you weigh in on this topic? Is it really possible . . . does it already exist . . . what conclusion have you arrived at in *your* mind and heart? This is an important question to ponder because your beliefs contribute to the "consciousness soup" which we are all concocting and serving to ourselves as well as future generations. In other words, irrespective of which way you may lean in this debate, it is nonetheless crucial that we as a species embrace the idea that we are all in this life together, and therefore, what affects one of us affects all of us. We are all citizens of this planet we call home. We share the same name—Human Being—and we breathe the same air and draw our food from the same source, Mother Earth. The questions are, does the world as we know it today *work* for you and everyone else on the planet as it is, or does something need to fundamentally change for that to occur? And, if it does, are you willing to be the change that is needed? Perhaps the answers depend on your personal vision *of* and *for* the world.

Where there is no vision, the people perish.

~ PROVERBS 29:18

To perceive the world as it appears today and not be seduced into believing it is broken, while at the same time, holding a vision of the possibilities of what it can be tomorrow is a high calling—this is the work of a visionary. Some may consider it walking the razor's edge because there will always be those who are not able (or willing) to catch the vision and call those who hold such a vision dreamers, or worse. The skill lies in synthesizing the dream, converting it into a vision fueled with passion and a plan that in turn puts legs on it. Several years ago Centers for Spiritual Living (CSL) did just that when "A World That Works for Everyone" became its official vision. As a spiritual organization, it seems appropriate that CSL would embrace such a bold vision because the words—and the intention found in the essence of the words—have been a social meme floating around the planet for a very long time, and they deserve to be revisited, reenergized and given a new platform.

Over the years respected people in the human potential movement have embraced the same idea in one form or another; in the 1970s Buckminster Fuller and Werner Erhard spoke to this vision, in essentially the same words. In 1927, our founder and author of *The Science of Mind,* Dr. Ernest Holmes, shared what became known as the Declaration of Principles. In it he wrote, "We believe the ultimate goal of life to be a complete emancipation from all discord of every nature, and that this goal is sure to be attained by all." Do his words depict a vision of a world that works for everyone? I believe it is safe to say yes; note that he was very specific when he said, "to be attained by all." How are we to interpret this? "To be" would imply a specific intention assigned to some time in the future . . . and "attained by all" clearly leaves little wiggle room for conjecture; it means inclusive of every human being, not just a chosen fortunate few. The fact that Centers for Spiritual Living chose to give the essence of Holmes's statement in the Declaration of Principles renewed meaning and visibility to an entirely new generation of humankind says volumes about the intention, heart, and soul of the organization, its leaders, and what they teach.

In my estimation, Holmes was a visionary, and his words resonate as a potential vision statement for humankind. A vision first originates in one's mind and is seen as a *completed* idea long before it is fulfilled in the relative world; a visionary is one who lives *in the vision* even before others may perceive it. This is why visionaries have often been called dreamers. To them the embodiment of a world that works for everyone is exquisitely ubiquitous while at the same time, intensely personal because it leaves no one out. Such a vision points the way, inviting every human being to add his own unique gift to the mix—to live up to a higher ideal—to metaphorically bring heaven to earth in one form or another while at the same time, sensing it *already* exists as Infinite Potential. Clearly, a vision is where the seeds of a world that works for everyone are planted and begin to germinate in new ways.

Global Transformation Begins as an Inside Job

> If you want to awaken all of humanity, then awaken all of yourself. If you want to eliminate the suffering in the world, then eliminate all that is dark and negative in yourself. Truly, the greatest gift you have to give is that of your own self-transformation.
>
> ~ LAO TZU

Remembering the edict of the masters throughout history—"As within, so without . . . as above, so below"—perhaps we can find common ground by stating that a world that works for everyone *already* exists because we have called it out and given it a thought form, which is always the fore-runner of a condition. As metaphysicians we know that we are always becoming cause to our own effect; that for each of us, the creative process begins in our mind and heart and then—and *only* then—can it become manifest in our world. As Gary Zukav and Lao Tzu both infer, creating a world that works for everyone begins by transforming ourselves first—awakening to the Light of our own spiritual magnificence and then extending that Light to the world in a manner that honors and reflects our vision.

At the end of the day it becomes clear that, as my colleague and friend Temple Hayes stated at an Association for Global New Thought (AGNT) rally, "A world that works for every-one will become manifest only to the degree that it works *through* everyone." With mindfulness and equanimity, let us each explore the regions of our own mind and heart and discern which way we "lean" with the vision of a world that works for everyone. For some, just the thought of what it would take to create such a world will require a willingness to go where we, collectively as a species, have never been before; a world where reverence, selflessness, sharing, cooperation, compassion, non-judgment, and inclusiveness is the norm. Perhaps that world already exists for you, perhaps it doesn't. In either case, you may be assured there will always be space to expand *your personal vision*—to grow into and evolve it in ways that add something affirmative to the consciousness soup from which we all draw sustenance and meaning.

> If not you, who?
> If not now, when?
> If not here, where?
>
> ~ WERNER ERHARD

We are each visionaries because we each have the capacity to cast a vision in our mind and nurture it in our heart long before it becomes a reality in our outer world. We have each been visionaries our entire life; it is how we created the life we have and the world we see before us every day when we walk out our front door. What we choose to see in our world determines how we will respond to it. The vision we hold for our life and our world determines who we are as we walk through the door of our workplace, the post office or—for that matter—our home when we return to it at the end of a long day. The vision we hold colors the lens through which we see other people and events occurring around our world. With mindfulness our vision can become a divine filter through which every thought, word, deed, and action passes inspection before it is clothed in form, becoming part of the world we are co-creating with so many other conscious beings. A world that works for everyone is evolving—it is a work in progress, an idea whose time has come, and we each play a crucial role in its unfoldment. When all is said and done, we know there is really only One of us here. We also know where two or more are gathered in a vision of Oneness amazing things happen.

Can I Get a Witness?

Sometimes our best teachers

are not the ones we feel like bringing apples to . . .

The Mirror That Never Lies

> Have you noticed that when you look in the mirror and your hair is messed up you don't try to brush the mirror; wisdom guides you to brush your own hair.
>
> ~ DENNIS MERRITT JONES

Sometimes I amaze myself with how much more I have to learn about practicing what I have been "teaching and preaching" for more than thirty-three years. Occasionally I come across an individual with whom I have an instantaneous negative reaction—something arises within me that wants to get away from that person's energy immediately. This happened at a restaurant recently when I was seated at a table directly next to a person who was talking incessantly in an exceedingly loud, invasive, grating, penetrating voice that dominated the entire room. I am aware that this disturbed me because my soul is on a perpetual quest for peace and stillness, even when I am dining out.

Now here's the sticky part for me: according to "spirit-mind-body" authorities such as Deepak Chopra, the people in my life are serving as a mirrors that never lie, including that person in the restaurant. *Really?* What part of me could possibly be that way? OMG! After some serious self-inquiry it became clear that at times, the exceedingly loud, grating, penetrating voice that incessantly dominates the conversation while never taking a breath is the internal voice in my head, especially when I am trying to feed myself spiritually by meditating or reading a complex passage in a book. The takeaway for me is to pay more attention to that voice and learn better how to make peace with it rather than react to it with irritation, unsuccessfully trying to push it away or avoid what it is saying. When I do listen and gently acknowledge it, it quiets down all on its own. Go figure—what you resist, persists.

The moral of the story is, when I am willing to catch myself red-handed in the judgment of others, realizing that ultimately the person whom I am really judging is myself, the awareness I need most comes flooding in. The lesson is, the more a person offends me, the deeper the trigger point lies within myself. If it were not so, that person's presence would have no effect upon me whatsoever. What a great opportunity every person offers me—to heal some aspect of my own being when I am open, aware, and teachable. Well now that I have told on myself, how about you; who do you project your less than desirable traits on? As an example, maybe your teacher is the person standing on the corner with a sign asking for money, which offers you an opportunity to get in touch with how you feel about sharing your good with others, or a perhaps a fear about lack in your own life you don't want to face. The lessons will vary because our teachers are legion; every human being is our potential teacher if we are willing to receive the lesson he brings to us. If we are open and paying attention, the right teacher always seems to appear at the right moment.

In those moments of ego projection, if we are willing to take a deep breath and peek into our mind we may be stunned by the findings. Remaining open to being taught by someone who by our judgment, is offensive or somehow not behaving in a manner we think he should, is not always easy, but it is possible. When we have the courage to stay the course of conscious self-inquiry with a willingness to learn the lesson at hand, the barriers usually melt away, our judgment dissolves, and we receive that understanding about ourselves which our teacher offers.

Give thanks for your master teachers each day. You will discover any projection usually centers on a need to love yourself and others more, and judge yourself and others less. As a mindfulness practice today, become the observer of your thoughts and judgments about others. Don't allow any thought, positive or negative, about another to slip by unnoticed. When that person offers you a rare glimpse into yourself, smile and silently say, "Thank you." Take the lesson and see how it applies in your life. Remember, *you* are also a reflection in *their* eyes. May they realize that the gentle and loving Spirit they see in you is but a reflection of their own divine nature.

THE MIRROR NEVER LIES.

It has long been said that Earth is the greatest school of all and life itself the only real curriculum—this means that class is always in session.

Earth School Is Open– Are Our Minds?

> Earth School: A special learning environment in which all that needs to be examined and brought to health in each individual is revealed to her or him in the intimacy of her or his personal experience.
>
> ~ GARY ZUKAV

On the day we are born we enter the "Earth School" (a term coined by my friend and colleague Gary Zukav) not knowing a thing. The soul may come overflowing with wisdom accumulated along the eternal journey, but the intellect is a blank slate. As we mature chronologically, emotionally, and spiritually, advancing in our understanding of the rules of living in a human skin, the message we are given is that the more we evolve, the more we need to know. If we are to live fully connected to meaning and purpose we must continue to explore life and unfold our minds. This means, irrespective of our age, we shall never reach a point where we can stop learning. Enrollment in Earth School is open to everyone. The tuition is the spiritual coin of one's energy, time, intention, and attention.

The only prerequisite for enrollment is an open mind that knows there is more to know, and a willingness to step into the unknown, over and over again. There are no age restrictions in Earth School and it is only through the portal of one's own curiosity, inquisitiveness, courage, commitment, and faith can one continue to advance.

Learning happens only when we step out of our box called the "known."

Metaphorically, many of us live our entire lives in a box. There is much comfort to be found in the confines of a box when we know where the edges are—but there is certainly no growth, no evolution, no deepening of our spiritual nature. It's frightening to step into the unknown, yet that is where learning and new creation takes place. If in the creative process, we use only our past as a reference point for our future, we just create more of what we have already created, another version of the same thing. It is nothing more than the Law of Cause and Effect at work. If we desire to create a new experience, we must introduce a new cause, and new causes will never be found in past experiences.

This reality creates a conundrum—to learn more we must be willing to leave the zone of the known and step into the void. Each time we advance in school, from the first grade all the way through high school and perhaps college, we are repeatedly required to enter through doors of uncertainty, trusting we will be provided with whatever we need to progress to our next stage of growth. Then things change. As we mature into adulthood we get quite comfortable in the relative known. This is also when "stuck-in-the-rut-itis" sets in. (Someone once defined a rut as a grave with no ends.) So we settle in, and life on the merry-go-round begins. We know exactly where it is going, and that would be nowhere. This is when a part of us begins to die. The rut is a grave—we just don't know it. No matter how far we may or may not go in school, the analogy applies. The ultimate school is life itself. From the day we are born—when we enter the mystery of not knowing—until the day we leave the planet, the only way to grow is to step into the unknown time after time, where new lessons await us.

The key to learning lies in the unknown, and curiosity and inquisitiveness unlock that door.

Curiosity is the desire to learn about anything—it invites us to venture beyond the boundaries of what we already know. Just watch any two-year-old child and you will see what I mean. Curiosity is energized by the spirit within that knows there is more to know, and the only way of learning what that is, is to follow its lead. I have a great master teacher by the name of "Mac Doodle." He is a seven-year-old Labradoodle. It doesn't matter what mission he is on, whether it's fetching the ball or just running wildly through the yard, he will often stop on a dime, turn, and begin intensely sniffing the scent of some mysterious creature, or chase an errant windblown leaf, or follow the sound of something into the bushes. His ability to be fearlessly curious about life in the moment seems to come naturally.

By the time Master Mac was four months old he had explored every square inch of our back yard and was becoming a bit bored with it all. Then I took him on his first walk through the neighborhood and he nearly went berserk with excitement —every sense he had was instantly alive with curiosity and wonder—he had entered a whole new level of learning in Classroom Earth and he knew it. The only difference between Mac and you and me is that although he can be curious, he *can't* be inquisitive—we can. Inquisitiveness is the process of using our thinking mind, inquiring or asking questions that allow us to clarify, process, and absorb new information—it's a fast track to learning. Just like Mac, our ability to be curious is innate, we just have to access it and follow its lead. The good news is we can also ask questions along the way, which enhances deeper learning. Like Mac, we enter a whole new level of learning in Classroom Earth every time we walk out the front door—we need only be open to exploring the wonder of it all.

Courage and commitment allow us to lean into learning.

Another of my master teachers are birds. The only thing required for baby birds to soar to freedom beyond the confines of an enclosed little nest is the courage to come to the edge of everything they have ever known and lean into the call of gravity with commitment. It is this commitment that awakens the intelligence within the bird that knows how to fly; until that commitment is made, the "knowing how to fly" lies dormant.

A full commitment also means there is no turning back. And so it is with us.

Just like the birds, we were born fully equipped to break free of past confining conditions that no longer serve us and it is our destiny to do so. We were born to be free—to expand our horizons by going where we have never gone before. There is a place within you and me that is courageous beyond our human understanding. It knows how to fly, and it yearns to explore beyond the boundaries of our daily life. Are we paying attention to that call, or are we resisting its nudge toward the edge, afraid to lean over?

Ernest Holmes referred to that inner impulse to push out as "the Divine Urge." It could be said that the Divine Urge permeates every living thing, and its voice perpetually whispers in our ear: "Grow, grow, grow . . . I have to be more tomorrow than I was yesterday." But there is another voice that often is much louder—the voice of fear. It shouts, "No, no, no . . . stay, stay, stay! Stay right where you are because while you may not like it, at least you know the rules and the boundaries. It is safe, and you risk nothing by staying put." That is the big lie, however—there is *great* risk in resisting the Divine Urge to grow.

A Universal Imperative: Grow or Die

It is a universal imperative that all living things must grow, and if they don't, they will die. There is no middle ground. When we cease growing, a part of us begins to slowly die—physically, emotionally, and spiritually. When our body stops growing it starts to wither. When our relationships stop growing they begin to stagnate and die; the same is true for our career and everything else that needs the life force to sustain homeostasis, vibrancy, and health.

The earthbound part of us cherishes the illusion that there is security in knowing what the future holds. Attachment to this illusion keeps us stuck in the zone of the known as we succumb to its voice of seeming logic and reason. The minute we yield to that voice and make the fear-based choice to settle for our current conditions, an intangible but vital part of us begins to wither and die because its purpose is not being honored. That part of us is our soul. For proof of this you need look no further than to those who choose to stay in a relationship or job long after the soul—the life force that originally brought it passion and joy—has vacated the premises. Our soul's nature (like the universe) is to evolve and push out, ever finding greater ways to express the Life we have been given. This expansion requires leaving the comfort of the known and continuing our education in Classroom Earth—forever learning, forever growing and knowing there will always be more to know.

Learning anything new requires patience and faith.

The process of learning anything new requires time, discipline, and, perhaps most important, patience. Too often we retard our own growth because we seek instant gratification, trying to learn faster than we can embody the learning.

We did not create the consciousness that currently defines our life in an eight-week course, but rather over a period of many years by embodying new beliefs, one at a time. Slow and steady wins the race of learning.

Again turning to nature, we witness the wisdom of patience working at every level. As a mindfulness practice, sit in a garden and allow the plants to be your teacher. You'll never hear a rose bush grunt and strain, trying to force its buds to open. There is wisdom within the rose that knows when it's time to unfold. Likewise, we can't force ourselves to grow faster than we should, any more than we can force a rose to blossom. However, we can have faith that the same Life force that opens the rosebud at the perfect time is also operating through us, and It knows when to open us as well. We can learn to pace ourselves, understanding that growth of any kind requires a cycle of the seasons, some of light, others of darkness, each with its own rhythm and purpose. Our job is to align with God's Presence, patiently stay the course, and remain conscious, taking action when guided, knowing in faith that in Classroom Earth, Life always knows how to sustain itself with grace and ease when we do our part.

We must trust we live in a universe that holds unlimited potential for us and is guiding us to that potential. But the only way we can receive that guidance is to open ourselves to it by saying, "I know there is more to know," and by being present in the moment and listening to Infinite Intelligence—the same Intelligence that gives birth to new stars, planets, galaxies, puppies, and roses. It is waiting to help us give birth to a new idea of what makes a life worth living. Clearly we have a role to play in giving birth to that idea. A plethora of learning opportunities present themselves to us every day. The Internet and bookstores are overflowing with material containing inspired ideas for learning, and many of the Centers For Spiritual Living are always offering new classes of a wide variety. Every moment invites us to learn something new; every person, event, and circumstance offers us a lesson that will enrich our lives if we are open and teachable.

Classroom Earth is in session now and there is a desk with your name on it. Enter consciously with an open mind.

WHAT YOU LEARN
WILL BE A BLESSING TO YOU
AND YOUR WORLD.

Our fears can erect invisible walls that keep our soul essence compressed and unexpressed. This can lead only to a life of dissatisfaction and regret.

How to Let Your **Inner Elvis Out**

It's all right to have butterflies in your stomach. Just get them to fly in formation.

~ DR. BOB GILBERT

Years ago I remember reading an interview with Elvis Presley. It was well known that beneath the stage act of his sexy machismo and bravado, Elvis had a softer side that was relatively fearful and insecure. When asked if he ever got nervous before his performances, he replied that in his early days he was so afraid that he would nearly always throw up just before going on stage. What if he had given in to his fear of performing and hadn't shared his unique gift? He might have ended up doing something with his life that would have been far less rewarding for him, as well as his millions of future fans. The irony is, in his wake he left countless others who created an industry of trying to emulate him rather than find their own center of uniqueness within. Even though in his later years he definitely had his share of demons to dance with, over the span of his career he nonetheless defined and redefined himself a number of times, and each iteration was as original as the one before. Because of that, his memory lives on in the hearts and minds of millions of people.

We don't have to be famous rock stars to relate with this story.

For many of us, fear is no stranger when it comes to stepping out of our comfort zone and onto the stage of a new experience to share the gift of ourselves with the world and more fully express who we really are in our daily lives. Anytime we follow the pathway that honors our authentic self it is likely that fear will be part of the experience. Too often, however, we end up standing comatose in the wings just offstage because we allow our fear of failure (or sometimes, success) or our fear of being judged and rejected to keep us there.

For some of us, stepping onto the stage may mean dealing with the fear of applying for a new job that more fully honors who we really are, or feeling the butterflies within fluttering madly as we ask someone on a first date while at the same time trying not to be anyone other than who we authentically are. Then again, it could also mean grappling with the fear of losing or leaving a longtime job or relationship. Anything that pushes us onto the stage where we are forced to confront and transcend our fear of being is when the portal to our redefining moments open and avail themselves to us if we are willing to step through them.

If we are not mindful, the fears that linger within will define our lives for us without our conscious consent or awareness. Our fears erect invisible walls that keep us and our soul essence compressed and unexpressed, and this can lead only to a life of dissatisfaction and regret. Why? Because we inherently know, beyond the fear, something within us that is larger than the fear is calling us to step up and into the limelight of a life worth living: it is the authentic self seeking the freedom to be what it came here to be. We know it is there—we can feel its presence and desire to be set free. Perhaps the only real difference between us and the young Elvis is that along with sensing that presence, he also allowed himself to feel the fear, throw up, and then get on with what he knew he was born to do. We could say he learned to let his inner Elvis—his authentic self—out. Even though too often we tend to feel the fear and hold back, the good news is it's never too late to let our own inner Elvis out as well.

The practice is to acknowledge our fear and embrace it rather than deny or run from it. Embracing our fear means to make a conscious choice to not allow it to define who we are or what we can accomplish. The energy of fear, once harnessed, can be like a highly spirited racehorse we can ride to our own greatness. What did Elvis know that perhaps we may not know? He knew he had to saddle that horse night after night, mount up and hold on tight to the dream he had come here to make his reality.

It's all right to have fear in your life—just be willing to ride it rather than run from it.

YOU'LL BE AMAZED
WHERE IT CAN TAKE YOU WHEN
YOU HOLD THE REINS.

What kind of God did you grow up with?
This is an important question because it will determine the quality and content of your life.

Up Close and Personal with **"The Thing Itself"**

All men seek some relationship to the Universal Mind, the Oversoul, or Eternal Spirit, which we call God.

~ ERNEST HOLMES, *THE SCIENCE OF MIND*

I remember as an enthusiastic spiritual neophyte exploring the teachings of Ernest Holmes, opening *The Science of Mind* textbook the first time to the very first chapter and seeing its title, "The Thing Itself." It put an immediate smile on my face. I had an instant flashback to the 1951 sci-fi thriller that I'd seen as a kid: *The Thing*, about an alien creature who crash-landed on planet Earth. At first I caught myself chuckling, and then I realized I was absolutely hooked by, and enchanted with, the idea that this spiritual genius would refer to God as "The Thing."

While clearly Dr. Holmes was not writing about a space alien, he was writing about a concept that was then, and still is, alien or foreign to many people. To imagine God as a *nonjudgmental,* Omnipotent, Omniscient, Omnipresent, Creative Principle —the Infinite Intelligence of a spiritual Universe, expressing, expanding, and revealing Itself in, through, and as Its creation

—has profound implications, How "on earth" might we ever have a personal relationship with such a *Thing*?

It got me thinking: Why would he use the term *The Thing Itself* as our first introduction to Science of Mind and our relationship with God? Could it be that he wanted us to enter the teaching with no preconceived ideas about "God" that might then limit our experience of the spiritual Wholeness in which he so deeply believed?

The word "God" can mean entirely different things to different people—be it good or not-so-good. Perhaps better said, the word "God" can become a label we place on our idea of what, in reality, is absolutely indescribable in Its "Allness." Whenever we place a label on anything we are defining it according to our own personal history, standards, preferences, prejudice, and opinions. In the process of categorizing it, we limit or restrict our experience of it because we have predetermined what it is or isn't. Dr. Holmes understood this and was in essence saying, that which is Infinite *can't* be restricted. While even the term *The Thing Itself* is a label, it allows us to approach a larger idea of a Universal Presence with an open mind because the word "thing" can mean, well . . . *any*thing. Perhaps this is what Dr. Holmes had in mind when he encouraged us to "remain open at the top."

Irrespective of the name by which we refer to It, the one thing most of us have in common is that from the time human beings first stood upright we have sought an understanding of God, what It is, how It works and, most important, how to have a relationship with It that gives our lives a sense of safety, freedom, happiness, fulfillment, inner peace, purpose, and meaning. There is a marvelous, elegant, sequential unfolding of Spirit that reveals Itself naturally as we evolve in our understanding of *The Thing Itself*. As we remain steadfast in our quest to personalize and deepen our relationship with God, one day we awaken to the fact that, as Dr. Holmes put it, "What we are looking for, we are looking with." In other words, the deeper we delve into our relationship with It, the more fully we experience our oneness, not only *with* It, but also as It, and all sense of separation *from* It is dissolved.

Taking the big leap makes us Whole.

The leap from *with* It, to *as* It, is a big one, and yet it is this leap in faith that literally makes us Whole because it fully unifies us with the Wholeness from which we have come. To make this point more succinctly, my version of the Creation Story goes something like this: In the beginning there was only God . . . and there still is *only* God, period, end of sentence. To take this idea a bit deeper, in the beginning there was only God, the Infinite One, and It so fully desired to know, experience, and express Its own Divine Nature that the only way It could do this was to think Itself into a multitude of forms and clothe Itself as those forms—which are you and me and everything we can or *can't* see, touch, hear, taste or smell. It is the guiding Intelligence that gives birth to babies and galaxies. From the air we breathe, and the atoms, protons, molecules, and cells that are the building blocks of life, to the bumblebees and begonias in our garden and the sun and moon in the sky—from the planet we call home, to the furthest galaxy on the very edge of a universe expanding at the speed of light, *and beyond,* It is *The Thing Itself* . . . the All that is. The question is, how do we make that leap from wishing, hoping, or trying to be one *with* It, to knowing we *are* It? To fully embody the awareness that we are each individuated points of Divine expression in such an expansive Universe can be overwhelming. To get up close and personal with "All that is" requires a delicate balance of logic and faith, understanding that, while we are not all that God is, God is most definitely all that we are. The question remains, how do we even approach such a "Thing" to find *our unique place* in Its vast Allness?

We begin by identifying the kind of God we grew up with and, if necessary, depersonalizing it.

For more than thirty years I have been privileged to introduce new students to the teachings of Dr. Holmes and Science of Mind, my goal has been to help them empty out their minds and release old concepts and attachments that they may have to a God that is whimsically unpredictable, and whose favor can be bought with enough begging, bargaining, and beseeching. I challenge them to take an unbiased look at the concept of God they currently hold. Sometimes the old beliefs regarding the God we grew up with still linger in the shadows of our unconscious mind unbeknownst to us. Many of us were raised believing in a "sky God"—an ancient-looking old man with a long white beard who magically existed somewhere "out there" just beyond the canopy of stars above. "He" held a lightning bolt in one hand and a logbook in the other, watching our every move, taking names and notes, tracking our every thought, deed, and action. We would generally assign a male gender and a personality to this version of God that is sometimes loving and benevolent—sometimes judgmental and punitive, based on our current or past behavior. With enough supplication we might then be invited to climb onto His gigantic lap and feel loved, approved of, and at peace, that is, until the next time we fell out of grace with Him. What kind of relationship might we ever hope to have with this sort of God, other than one based on a belief in separation, held firmly in place by a lifetime of fear, guilt and shame?

My point is this: As odd as it may sound, before we can have an intimate, personal, and loving relationship with *The Thing Itself* we may have to first *depersonalize* God and see It not as a personality, but rather as a Universal, Omnipresent Principle which treats us all the same by operating impersonally and impeccably through the Law of Cause and Effect. This idea alone shatters the crystalized image that has held countless people hostage for thousands of years to a sky God that rules His Kingdom with favoritism, wrath, and judgment. We want to see and experience God as a loving Presence, and we shall if we stay the course. However, without first understanding God as impersonal Law, the Universe and how It operates in our daily lives will make little sense to us. Once we understand the nature of how It works as Law we can then begin to experience the nurturing aspect of God as the unconditioned Love It is.

> The great Love of the Universe must be One with the great law of Its Own Being, and we approach Love through the Law. This then is the teaching: Love and Law. As the Love of God is perfect, so the Law of God also is perfect. We must understand both.
>
> ~ ERNEST HOLMES, *THE SCIENCE OF MIND*

Why is it so important to understand the Universal Law of Cause and Effect? To paraphrase Dr. Holmes, while the Love of God may point the way to a life worth living, it is the Law of God that makes the way possible. Our lives are a perfect commingling of Love and Law. We use the Law of Cause and Effect every day by means of our thinking, or to be more specific, our beliefs, which lead to the choices we make and the resulting actions we take. In this manner we are continually becoming cause to our own effect. We know that God is Love in Its highest vibration because we are given absolute freedom to shape and reshape our destiny, depending on how consciously we choose to use the Law. Only Infinite unconditional Love could offer us the freedom to choose and then choose again, and thus set ourselves free by affirmatively using the very same impartial Law that, until we are conscious of It, holds us in bondage. This is *The Thing Itself,* the creative principle, in action: Love and Law working together—each perfect in the gift It brings to the process of co-creation. It becomes obvious why having an intimate relationship with *The Thing Itself* is so vital to our sense of wholeness and well-being: Love (as conscious free will) does indeed point the way, and the impartially of the Law makes it possible. Our ability to personalize *The Thing Itself* gives us an authentic sense of connection to both the Love and the Law of God.

Personalizing our relationship with The Thing Itself means finding the way back to the core of our being and connecting with our own Divinity in human ways.

Perhaps the greatest lesson ever given to us regarding the duel nature of God came from the great teacher Jesus. He understood the necessity of internalizing God and having an intimate relationship with the universal principles of both Love and Law. He was a master at guiding people to their own Divinity in ways in which they could relate. Talking about labels, he referred to "The Thing" as "The Father" because he knew the people of his time and culture could *personally* relate to the image of a father. No doubt, in such a patriarchal society, the father of the household was greatly loved and held in high esteem because he was the provider of all his family's needs, and he did so with love. In addition, his "word" was respected as the law of the household. There it is; the perfect metaphor to illustrate the principle of Love and Law in a language his followers could relate to.

At the end of the day the essence of Jesus's teachings can be boiled down to two statements with which we can all relate, and they perfectly describe *The Thing Itself,* how It works, and how to get up close and personal with It. First, he said, "It is done unto you as you believe" (Matt 8:13). How the Law of God works has never been more clearly stated: If we don't like what is going on in our lives (the effect) it may be time to take a look at our deepest beliefs (the cause) *about* life, remembering we are always becoming cause to our own effect. Second, he said, "The Kingdom of God is within you" (Luke 17:21). Never has the case for our oneness with, in, and as God been stated so succinctly: We don't have to "earn" God's Love, because we are immersed in it already—It is in us and, even more so, we are in It, so much so that we have been "marinating" in Divine Love from the day we were conceived. The gift of the Life we have been given and the ability to freely express that Life as we choose is full proof of how much we are unconditionally loved by God. What we choose to do with our lives is the gift we offer back to the giver.

Irrespective of what you may call It, may you always maintain the ability to have a personal relationship with *The Thing Itself.* May you always be in awe of Its expansive and unlimited creative nature and seek new ways to deepen and personalize your relationship with It. Most important, may you never lose sight of the fact that God is embedded in the core of your being, or as Dr. Holmes said, your mind and spirit are your echo of the *Eternal Thing Itself.*

MAY THAT ECHO REVERBERATE FOREVER
AND BE THE INFALLIBLE BEACON THAT LEADS YOU
HOME IN THOSE TIMES WHEN YOU FORGET
WHO YOU REALLY ARE.

Many people are addicted to instant gratification and because of this they cheat themselves out of one of life's most rewarding experiences: the ability to witness one's own creative process.

The Wisdom of **Patience**

Good character is not formed in a week or a month. It is created little by little, day by day. Protracted and patient effort is needed to develop good character.

~ AUTHOR UNKNOWN

A martial arts student went to his master teacher and said earnestly, "I am devoted to learning your art form. How long will it take me to obtain the highest degree black belt?" The teacher's reply was casual, "Ten years." Impatiently, the student answered, "But I want to master it faster than that. I will work very hard. I will practice with great effort every day, ten or more hours a day, every day, if I have to. How long will it take then?" The teacher thought for a moment and said, "In that case, it will take twenty years."

Because impatience has been my longtime nemesis, this ancient teaching parable quickly came to mind as I sat behind the potter's wheel for my first ceramics class. I have reached a point in my life where it has become apparent it's time to find a few new creative outlets that continue to stimulate my growth and feed me with a sense of accomplishment. What I learned instantly from my ceramics teacher, Esther, is there is no such thing as instant gratification in making a bowl on the wheel. Being a recovering "type A" person, the first words out of her mouth were just what I did NOT want to hear: "Now this is going to require some patience." While my inner mindfulness-meditation teacher took a deep breath and smiled, silently affirming, "But of course it will," that ten-year-old boy trapped in this man's body was clamoring to get his hands into the sticky, muddy clay and go for it ASAP with abandon. With Esther's calm guidance, as the wheel started spinning I centered my clay and opened it in the middle. So far so good. Then as I started to quickly lift the edge of the bowl, applying equal pressure from both the inside and outside with two fingers, the thin wall of the bowl started wobbling and Esther again calmly admonished me to slow down and have patience because if I went too fast the fragile clay would fly apart. The good news is, slow and steady won the race and my first bowl was born.

Admittedly, I was very impressed with myself until Esther said, "Nice work! Next week you can do step two." Next week . . . step two? You mean I have to wait until NEXT week to get to step two? OMG! Was she saying I had more to learn, more time to wait before I could take "my" bowl home and put some chips and guacamole in it? No doubt patience was a lesson that had my name all over it so I took a deep breath and went home empty handed. Fast forward to the second week when I was taught to trim the bowl and sign my name on the bottom preparing it for its first firing. Then, more waiting. Now fast forward to week three when the bowl was painted, glazed and prepared for its final firing in the kiln. Lastly, jump ahead to week four when I FINALLY had the pleasure of munching on some chips directly from my newly finished creation. Whew! Delayed gratification is such a high price to pay for the privilege of learning and creating something new.

Can you relate? Where in your life might more patience be needed? While there is always room for improvement when it comes to having patience with other people, I am referring to the patience we have with ourselves. The first step is knowing that regardless of what we are endeavoring to learn, create, or achieve, patience is the connective tissue that unifies the beginning, middle, and the end of the process. I use the example of making pottery because clearly, a raw hunk of clay doesn't become a finished bowl on its own in one day, nor does a novice become a master of anything worth creating in one day. We could say that we are all students on the potter's wheel of life learning how to shape our lives. The key is to remember there is a timeline involved in any creative process that needs to be honored. Becoming a master of anything worth doing requires the wisdom of patience and it begins with our next breath . . . and then the next . . . and then the next, creating the spaciousness between breaths for the unfolding of our true passion, genius, and soul.

How do we best implement the wisdom of patience? Over time I have learned the mindfulness practice of "high involvement and low attachment." This means being highly involved in the moment with little or no attachment to the results, which may take time to unfold. This practice invites the mind and the body to be in the present moment at the same time which is where and when the bliss of being and doing joyfully intersect and commingle as our experience. That is what patience does: it invites us to embrace the moment and get our hands in that sticky, muddy clay called life and mindfully shape it in a manner that expresses who we authentically are. The good news is you don't have to be a ten-year-old kid to do that.

AND THAT
REALLY IS A BEAUTIFUL THING.

If your mind were a temple,
who would be determining what thoughts may enter?
Holding the High Watch is not
a part-time endeavor.

Stand Guard at the Temple Gate!

> Man would have no burdens if he kept [the] "High Watch toward The One"—if he always turned to God.
>
> ~ ERNEST HOLMES, *THE SCIENCE OF MIND*

Have you ever had unwelcome invasive thoughts pop into your head and take your mind hostage, dominating your focus of attention? If you are like most people the answer is yes. Usually those type of thoughts are negative, fear-based and attached to either the future or the past where a sense of powerlessness runs rampant. I recall a period in my life as a boy, and even as a young adult, when I was compulsively addicted to negative thinking. My mind could conjure up things to obsess about regardless of where I was or what I was doing. A constant barrage of fear-based thoughts consumed me, chasing me around like a dog pursuing a frightened rabbit into a burrow and keeping it imprisoned there. The reason I am telling you this is that years ago, thanks to my mother (who was my first spiritual teacher), I was taught a mindfulness practice that enabled me to observe and stop those invasive thoughts, and now, with great respect, I would like to pass her wisdom on to you.

I remember the day I told my mom that my mind was perpetually filled with worry, fear, anxiety, and a sense of dread; I paraphrase below what she said:

In ancient times, many cities erected tall towers along their perimeter in which watchmen were posted with the order to be constantly vigilant and observant—ensuring that the well-being of the citizens was safeguarded from invading forces or unwelcome visitors. Because they were elevated in their towers and on duty around the clock, they were literally holding the "high watch" allowing them to identify anyone approaching in time to close the gate, if necessary. Son, you must learn to stand guard at the temple gate and hold the high watch.

She went on to explain that the temple was my mind (both conscious and subconscious) and the guard at the gate was my ability to consciously observe and decide what thoughts I would allow to enter my mind and occupy space. She also said that once identified as "friend or foe," I could either turn it away or choose to welcome it through the gate.

This was my first lesson in mindfulness. Years later I came to discover that New Thought pioneers such as Emma Curtis Hopkins and Ernest Holmes knew and taught the importance of holding the high watch—with the added understanding that it is not only a mental exercise but a spiritual practice as well. Working from the New Thought premise that God is all there is, the "watchman" signifies an awakened state of awareness of God's presence and the "watchtower" signifies an elevated and sustained state of consciousness. With clear intention, when we hold the high watch we see only the presence of God—irrespective of the unwelcome conditions we may be contending with in the moment. If we wish to be free of repetitive negative thought patterns and conditions we must learn to hold the high watch over our thoughts with absolute spiritual authority knowing that when we say "Halt—you are not welcome here," the Creator of the Universe supports that decision.

What a powerful way to see ourself, as a self-appointed guard, mindfully monitoring the invading or unwelcome thought forces trying to enter our head and denying them entry. To realize we are in command of our mind (and therefore our life) is immensely empowering and liberating. Easy to say but difficult to do? Certainly. Let us not be naive to think this is a practice we can master overnight; that is why it's called a practice. The habit-mind is a slow learner and it gains traction with repetition—but with time it can be trained to be our servant rather than our master. But what is the principle that will support us in retraining our mind to hold the high watch? In his classic book *Creative Mind,* Ernest Holmes points the way:

> No living soul can demonstrate two things at the same time, if one contradicts the other. There is no way except to let go of all that you do not wish to come into your experience, and, in mind, take all that you do wish. SEE, HEAR, TALK ABOUT, AND READ ONLY WHAT YOU WISH. AND NEVER AGAIN LET A NEGATIVE THOUGHT COME INTO YOUR MIND.

Standing Guard at the Temple Gate Means Being Single-Minded

Let's be honest with ourselves. Most of us have allowed our minds to doze off while on duty at the temple gate; our attention is so easily diverted and seduced by the collective consciousness—by even the smallest impulse of fear-based thinking—that it has become the norm. One might begin to wonder if it is even possible to maintain a focus solely on what is right and good. Our minds are constantly being bombarded with less than uplifting news, movies, magazines, video games, and so on, and as a result, an endless army of negative thoughts and feelings comes stealthily marching through the gate unnoticed.

The ancient admonition, "A house divided always falls," points the way to our first rule of engagement: We must take a stand for oneness in the presence of God and never compromise, never deviate, and never lose faith. This may be easier said than done *until* we realize that, as pointed out by Ernest Holmes, our minds are essentially "monophonic." This is good news! It means we can focus our attention on only one thing (or thought) at a time; with mindfulness and great discernment we can choose what that one thing (or thought) shall be, one moment, one breath at a time. This is how we train new recruits (higher thoughts) to man the watchtower. Perhaps it's time to become far more diligent regarding what thought impulses we allow to enter and dwell in our temple . . . but where do we begin?

A Call to Action

You might consider this your call to action—a time to take your mind to basic training at Camp Consciousness where you learn a new way of thinking; one that focuses *first and foremost* on your oneness with God. Let us also remember there may be times when we may need some support (reinforcements) in holding the high watch of oneness. Because we are all in this thing called Life together, once we have mastered the art of holding the high watch for ourselves we can then do so for others when requested. Not that we should try to stand guard at their temple gate—because we can't—that's an inside job only they can do. However, with great discernment we can hold them in prayer, affirming their oneness with God in those times when they are not able to do so for themselves. This is what holding the high watch means—training your mind to remember God's presence at the center and circumference of life; to think *up* when the world around you may be transfixed in thinking *down*. To assist you in training your mind to stand guard at the temple gate, here are several mindfulness practices that will help reinforce your ability to hold the high watch of oneness.

- **Pray Without Ceasing:** There is no wrong time to pray. Because it connects us directly to the Presence, the act of mindful prayer is one of the most natural ways to hold the high watch. Train your mind to see God's presence everywhere at all times and you'll discover that your life will become a living prayer. Take time daily to meditate and dwell in the presence of the Beloved and you'll know you stand not alone in your quest to hold the high watch.

- **Seek a Prayer Partner:** There are times when we all need "reinforcements" to stand guard at the temple gate with us—to hold us in a prayer of oneness when we may not have the clarity of mind to do so for ourselves. Ask someone of a like-mind to become your prayer partner, someone you can call on when you aren't able to hold the high watch for yourself and allow him the honor of serving you. Where two or more are gathered in spiritual agreement there is great power.

- **Be Mindful When Your Inner Guard Dozes Off:** You can be the observer of your own thoughts, and challenge and change the ones that don't serve you in a healthy manner—but it requires great discipline to do so. Take time daily to sit with your thoughts and observe where they want to take your mind. Be mindful of the visitors you allow to pass through the sacred gate to the temple. Always remember that you are in charge, you are the watch commander, and only you have the authority to invite in—or turn away—the visitor at the gate.

When we can create a healthy and proactive way to train our mind to focus on the presence of God (good) revealing Itself in and through *all* that we say, think, and do, we shall be living a spiritually integrated life—a life that is founded in our oneness with that which knows no opposition. As Paul states in Romans 8:31, "What then shall we say of these things? If God be for us, who can be against us?" That is an extraordinary thing to remember when holding the high watch of oneness.

LIFE IS GOOD AT THE TEMPLE GATE.

To live with reverence is to walk a sacred earth;
it touches everything you say, think, and do.
Living with reverence is not a one-day-a-week religious
act or ritual; it is a way of life.

Living Life with **Reverence**

> By having a reverence for life, we enter into a spiritual relation with the world. By practicing reverence for life we become good, deep, and alive.
>
> ~ ALBERT SCHWEITZER

In Southern California where I used to live we were blessed with year-around weather that encouraged growth of just about anything planted in the ground. With the rain and 75-degree days there is a preponderance of green showing up everywhere. As I sat peacefully in my meditation garden one morning, my eyes were drawn to some weeds that were beginning to pop up among my beautiful lilies and bamboo. My first inclination was to pull them out because I didn't want weeds to encroach upon and spoil the "perfectly groomed sacred space" I had dedicated to my meditation practices.

Thankfully, before I could act, that ever-present quiet voice within gently whispered, "Be still and know, this too is sacred." So I sat with the weeds and invited them to be my teacher. What was it I could learn about myself and life from the intrusion of a few errant weeds in my meditation garden? Emerson was on to something when he said that a weed was a plant whose virtues have not yet been discovered. Perspective is everything. In an instant, what had one moment earlier been perceived as an inconvenient, unsightly nuisance, instantly became another opportunity to practice reverence.

It was then that I recalled something I heard Dr. William Hornaday share long ago regarding reverence. He told the story of how Ernest Holmes, the author of *The Science of Mind,* would on occasion dine with a vase of weeds on his dining room table. What great insight and wisdom he had. He considered it a beautiful reminder that the creative intelligence of Life flows equally through every living thing, and that the only real difference between a weed and a rose was the value we choose to place upon one over the other. Of course we can extend the same premise to every form of life, from snails to whales, and everything in between, including you and me and every human being on this planet.

Reverence is the act of seeing through the form and recognizing and honoring the divine Presence at its center as well as its circumference. In other words, to see the sacred in a weed can be a spiritual experience if we are willing to look beyond form and see the divine Essence therein. No less true, to see the sacred in ourselves can, likewise, be a spiritual experience. In either case the only thing required of us is to deepen our perception by dropping our judgments, which are the primary things that separate us from the awareness of our oneness with all of Life. The practice of reverence is how we transcend our judgments, which sets us free from the tyranny of the ego-self that thrives on fear and separation by labeling everything and everyone as good or bad, desirable or undesirable, right or wrong, and so on. When it comes to how we tend to place other people in these categories, Swami Vivekananda spoke with great elegance to the issue of reverence when he said, "The moment I have realized God sitting in the temple of every human body, the moment I stand in reverence before every human being and see God in him—that moment I am free from bondage, everything that binds vanishes, and I am free."

Is it easy to rise to Vivekananda's high call to practice reverence with every human being? It's fairly easy with those people we love, like, and respect. However, it can be a bit more challenging with many others, especially if they hold core values and beliefs that differ from our own. Between the political elections and a war-torn world, we don't have to look too far for ample opportunities to begin practicing reverence outside the circle of our comfort zone. While it may sound very idealistic, can you imagine a world where reverence is practiced by more and more people? Maybe so, maybe not; but there is nothing to say it can't start with you and me.

The takeaway for me is this: while we may prefer roses over weeds it doesn't mean one is more sacred than the other. The Divine imbues Itself equally in all living things, which includes each of us. What value shall we place on all that our eyes gaze upon today? Where might we begin the conscious practice of reverence? The ancient philosopher Pythagoras offers us the perfect place to start: "Above the cloud with its shadow is the star with its light. Above all things reverence thyself." In other words, above and beyond all appearances, opinions, and circumstances, know there is a light, a sacred Presence, within you. Recognize It, honor It, and revere It, and It will set you free to love the world. A spiritual experience awaits you in every moment of this day if you have eyes to see—and it begins in the mirror.

REVERENCE THYSELF FIRST,
REMEMBERING "AS WITHIN, SO WITHOUT,"
AND YOUR LIFE SHALL BECOME THE SACRED JOURNEY
YOU CAME HERE TO HAVE.

How can the truth set you free?
Your consciousness shapes the lens through which you see everything; it is always absorbing new information based on what you embrace as true.

The Only Way Out IS IN

In oneself lies the whole world and if you know how to look and learn, the door is there and the key is in your hand. Nobody on earth can give you either the key or the door to open, except yourself.

~ JIDDU KRISHNAMURTI

Once, in ancient times, there was a man who believed he was unfairly placed in an isolated, dark, dank prison cell. There he sat in the corner, separated from the world for months, feeling depressed, resentful, and sorry for himself. Each night after the guard fell asleep the man leaned against the cell door, pushing it with all his might, trying to force it open, but always to no avail. Then late one night after months of pushing, he dropped to his knees in defeat and mumbled a humble prayer to God saying, "Dear Lord, I tried everything I know to set myself free . . . I need some guidance . . . please, show me the way out." No sooner had the words departed his lips and a voice gently whispered in his ear, "Sometimes the way out is in." Suddenly, a strong summer wind billowed through the prison and blew the cell door inward, toward him, and it flung open. In his stunned disbelief he realized that each night before retiring, the guard had closed—but never locked—the door. The man simply hadn't been consciously aware enough to notice which way the door swung. He took a deep breath and wondered why he had so easily given so much of his power to the guard. The possibility that "in" might be the way "out" didn't exist in his mind because he was so busy resentfully pushing against the door. It never occurred to him stand back and gently pull it.

And so, out of the prison cell he quietly walked with a valuable lesson in hand: Be fooled not by appearances; never allow yourself to be held prisoner to conditions that have no power over you other than the power you give them—be willing to turn within and know therein lies the answer. The key is you—more succinctly, the key is your mind and your ability to be conscious, aware, and present enough in the moment to see what "appears" to be a problem through new eyes. In other words, the real key to freedom is your consciousness; it is always your consciousness that determines your fate because it filters your perception, which in turn shapes your reality. Sometimes the only way out really is in.

This story is my adaptation of an ancient teaching parable. Although the source of the original story is unknown, I embellished it to make the point that, irrespective of the problem which may have you feeling imprisoned, your consciousness is your key to freedom—the "master key" that fits the lock to *any* challenge you may encounter. "Seeing through new eyes" is a metaphor for having a shift in consciousness. If you are willing to see any problem through new eyes you will be set free. A resolution to the problem will be revealed because that is how consciousness operates IF it is free and clear of mistaken perceptions and false beliefs. It is important to understand that your current consciousness is more than your objective mental awareness; it *is the sum of everything* you ever believed and accepted to be the truth about yourself and life, placed in the invisible container called your conscious and unconscious mind. The point is, you've always had the power to set yourself free; the good news *and* bad news is that this power is neutral—it doesn't care how you use it. As Ernest Holmes wrote in *The Science of Mind,* "We are bound because we are first free, and the power which binds us is the only thing in the universe which can free us. Man already has, within himself, the key to freedom." The age-old adage, "as within, so without" is really quite accurate. The way *in* IS the way *out;* your inner beliefs cannot help but shape your outer circumstances.

Look, Listen, and Learn!

Many people are fooled by appearances. After being subjected to a condition not to their liking—just like our man in the story—they tend to react and vehemently push against the problem, and when it doesn't give way to their rant they hunker down in the muck and the mire of the circumstance, convincing themselves they are helpless. The pitfall of helplessness is that it eventually breeds hopelessness—the feeling of being out of control, stuck in the darkness of a frightening situation with nowhere to run. Driven by that feeling they then mindlessly rush to a conclusion—based on what appears to be —and build a story that justifies, reaffirms, and perpetuates the condition. The irony is, the entire time the freedom (the way out) they long for lies directly in front of them if they have the eyes—the consciousness—to see it. As Krishnamurti infers, the key is knowing how to look at what lies before you and learn from it, rather than being imprisoned by it. The operative words here are *look* and *learn;* to do so is to add new content to your consciousness by jettisoning your mistaken perceptions and false beliefs. The practice is to remember it's your consciousness that shapes the lens through which you see everything. Like a sponge, it is always *absorbing* new information based on what you embrace as true. Will a shift in consciousness magically change outer conditions? Perhaps so, perhaps not; but the one thing it will absolutely change is your perception—how you see the problem—which introduces a new cause which in turn will change your experience of it. A new cause must bring with it a new effect.

The key required to set you free is already in the lock. The key is your consciousness and the lock is your perception of the problem; either you see it as unsolvable, or something that has no power over you other than the power you choose to give it. In either case, you will be correct because the universal law of cause and effect will assist in making it your reality. The way *out* of your problem, whatever it may be, lies *within.*

We need only learn to mindfully step back, and rather than push against "what is," reframe the moment by taking a deep breath, turning within, and making space for a *new* awareness of what "can be" to be revealed. The practice is to be still and listen, to be observant and willing to learn, because within the problem (prison cell) lies the answer (key). Because the theme of this story is universal and timeless, it is safe to say that at some point, everyone has had—or will have—something that stands between themselves and the life they dream of which lies just on the "other side" of the invisible bars of their current belief system. With this in mind, I offer five mindfulness practices that will assist you in moving toward freedom:

1. **BE PRESENT IN THE MOMENT**: The very first step in setting yourself free is taken the instant you become present in the moment. Becoming aware in the moment is liberating because it allows you to see clearly what is happening—not only in your outer physical environment but also within your body and mind. Being present also sets the stage for practicing the Presence of the Power that will free you.

2. **GET OUT OF DENIAL**: It is impossible to set yourself free until you can first honestly acknowledge you are being held captive behind the invisible bars of your current consciousness. With awareness comes power; once you take ownership of the situation in which you are imprisoned, you empower yourself to do something about it. This is the beginning of seeing through new eyes. Just remember ABC: **A**wareness **B**uilds **C**onsciousness.

3. **CHALLENGE THE PROBLEM**: Courageously examine the beliefs you currently embrace and see if they correspond with your problem; it's a matter of cause and effect. If they do, you must challenge them. To challenge the problem that has held you captive means you are calling it out. Once you are present in the moment and out of denial you have automatically given notice to the "prison guard" (your current consciousness) that you know there is a way out—and you are taking your power back.

4. **BE OPEN FOR GUIDANCE**: Rather than wasting precious hours, days, weeks, months, and years of your life pushing against the problem (which gives it only more power) make the divine surrender—not to the outer condition but to the inner solution. Invoke the awareness of God's presence within and ask for guidance. Rather than saying "Show me the way out, God," say, "Show me the way in." Then be patient; step back, breathe, and wait for an opening in consciousness to appear—and it will. Then be willing to follow the guidance received.

5. **STAY CONSCIOUS**: After waking up, often the greatest challenge is remaining awake. The collective consciousness is very seductive and is continually trying to lull you back to sleep, into complacency, into an invisible prison cell of ambivalence. Remembering that your mind is a container for the beliefs which form your consciousness is a lifetime practice—be mindful of what thoughts and beliefs you allow to pass through the hallowed gates of your consciousness. Knowing how to look at what lies before you in any given moment determines what you shall see.

THE ONLY WAY OUT
TRULY IS IN.

When you crack a book and read something that rings the inner bell that vibrates down to the core of your self-knowing, there is a reason why that happens . . .

Of Course, **You ALREADY Knew** That!

'Tis the good reader that makes the good book; in every book he finds passages which seem to be confidences or sides hidden from all else and unmistakably meant for his ear; the profit of books is according to the sensibility of the reader; the profound thought or passion sleeps as in a mine, until it is discovered by an equal mind and heart.

~ RALPH WALDO EMERSON

I love Emerson's insights; I marvel at how he causes me to pause, look within, and think about things that might otherwise sneak right past me in the course of a day. To consider that I am equal in mind and heart to some of the profound teachers throughout history, as well as contemporary teachers I may read or even listen to, is a compelling thought. There are times when reading a book I get the feeling that the author is speaking directly to me and is reminding me of some deeply buried nugget of truth that already lies within me. It's as if his words awaken within me the same knowing and I say to myself, "Of course, I already knew that." It's not necessarily a transmission of knowledge as much as it is a lightning bolt of remembrance or self-knowing.

Often after delivering a keynote talk, people approach me and say, "You must have been reading my mind; that talk was just for me—I heard exactly what I needed to hear." I smile and respond, "No, actually it was just for me because it is what I needed to hear right now—you just happened to be present, listening in on the conversation I was having with myself. If you found relevance with what was said it's because you walked in here with the ideas already living within you—I just helped you remember and recognize them."

The reason I point this out is that the same is true for you, whether you know it or not. When you read (or hear) something that finds deep resonance with your soul it's not because you are receiving anything new; you are remembering something that you already know at some level. How can this be so? To quote master teacher Emerson one more time: "There is one mind common to all individual men. Every man is an inlet to the same and to all of the same.... What Plato has thought, he may think; what a saint has felt, he may feel.... Who hath access to this universal mind is a party to all that is or can be done, for this is the only and sovereign agent." To put it in the language of metaphor, we are all swimming in the same pool of Infinite Intelligence, sharing what Emerson refers to as one universal mind. What is known at one point of the pool can be known at any point in the pool—it just requires an opening in consciousness to be revealed. That opening happens when we read or hear something that hooks our attention; it is then that the knowing (or remembering) floods in and we get that familiar ah-ha feeling.

Give this some thought the next time you crack a book and read something that rings the inner bell that vibrates down to the core of your self-knowing. When you read my words, or any writer's words that find a home in your heart, know that you are not being told anything you don't already know; you are being reminded of how much you know that you didn't remember you already knew. You are also being reminded of how amazingly connected you are to something far greater than you ever imagined, which in turn, connects you directly with the source of your inspiration—the universal mind with which you are one. The practice is to remember, as Emerson stated, the profound thought or passion sleeps . . . until it is discovered by an equal mind and heart.

To consider that your mind and heart are equal to that of Jesus, Buddha, Confucius, Spinoza, Voltaire, Nietzsche, Pythagoras, Shakespeare, Thoreau, Plato, Socrates, Rumi, Emerson, Hopkins, Browning, Holmes, Fillmore, Eddy, Gibran, Tolle, Dyer,

Chopra, Oprah, or (fill in the blank) ___________, puts you in very good company, and that indeed is a worthy and profound bit of wisdom to contemplate.

OF COURSE,
YOU ALREADY KNEW THAT.

There is wisdom in the ancient admonition
"Be still and know."
The challenge is knowing what stillness
really is and where to find it.
Be assured, it is closer than you think.

Stillness

> When you lose touch with inner stillness, you lose touch with yourself. When you lose touch with yourself, you lose yourself in the world.
>
> ~ ECKHART TOLLE, *STILLNESS SPEAKS*

The great spiritual mystics have taught the importance of taking time to truly experience the presence of the Divine, and in some manner that makes it personal, intentionally deepening our daily relationship with that Presence. This has been the quest of humankind for countless millennia: to find the sacred passageway—the mystical portal—from ourselves to the Divine through which that relationship may be actualized in our daily lives. The challenge has been that it seems to be the nature of the human mind to overcomplicate the process and there are a plethora of ways in which we do so. For proof of this, consider the thousands of religions that have been established to assist us in gaining access to God, each declaring that the *only* way to have a relationship with the Divine is *through* them. The irony is we never have needed—nor shall we ever need—anyone or anything to give us access to God because we *already* have access; we may just not be aware of that fact because of the many distractions that come with living in a human skin. As Tolle infers, we lose ourselves in the world because the seductive drama on the surface of life is always drawing our attention outward rather than inward toward our own sacred center.

In his classic book, *The Science of Mind,* Dr. Ernest Holmes made this very point with his typical eloquence when he wrote, "Spiritual experience is deep, calm and self-assertive; it is the result of actually realizing that Presence which binds all together in one complete Whole. This experience comes in the stillness of the Soul, when the outer voice is quiet, when the tempest of human strife is abated; it is a quickening of the inner man to an eternal reality." My sense is that Holmes is reminding us that we couldn't be any more "spiritual" because we are already 100 percent spirit; we are always marinating in Divine Essence. The only thing we can do is become more *aware* of this truth, and spirituality is the means by which this happens.

What Is Spirituality, Really?

> Theologians may quarrel, but the mystics of the world speak the same language.
>
> ~ MEISTER ECKHART

The language Meister Eckhart is referring to is spirituality, and it is a language we all can speak because it takes us beyond any words, doctrines, dogma, judgments, opinions, and rules and into the experiential realm of Oneness. Spirituality guides us to a point of deep self-awareness that transcends the perceived gap between ourselves and God, and thus, between our minds and our hearts and our souls and our bodies, creating the space for the mystical experience that awaits us. A mystic is simply one who perceives the presence of God beyond the veil of the five senses and *actualizes* It as a direct experience in the present moment. When we can cut through all the theological jargon found in religiosity we'll see that we can all be mystics when we understand that spirituality is merely the *intentional* practicing of God's presence—not just *in* our lives, but *as* our lives—at the center *and* circumference of our being, and not just on Sunday mornings and special occasions, but in every moment of every day. In the Zen tradition, there is a statement that speaks beautifully to how living in this sacred continuum is accomplished: "Before enlightenment, chop wood and carry water. After enlightenment, chop wood and carry water." Nothing has to change in the activity of our daily lives but our awareness of our oneness with the Presence in the moment.

The practice is to remember there is as much of Infinite Presence within us and around us when we are pulling weeds, washing the dishes, walking the dog, stuck in gridlock traffic, closing a business deal, feeding the baby, or in hospice care, as there is in the most sacred, high and holy temple, ashram, mosque, or church on the planet. To have this realization is to initiate the quickening of our inner being to an eternal reality which opens the portal to—as Holmes says—the Presence that binds all together in one complete Whole. In other words this "quickening" can innately manifest as a mystical experience in any given moment! He makes it sound so easy doesn't he? While it is exquisitely *simple* it is not always easy because it requires something of us that seems counterintuitive to our postmodern lifestyle of do, do, do. It requires us to be, be, be . . . to slow down, *be still,* and know we are literally immersed in Wholeness —in the Presence of God. The quintessential question is how do we find the fulcrum or pivot point between our doing and being in our daily lives and remain there? Martial artist Bruce Lee pointed out this quagmire when he said, "The stillness in stillness is not the real stillness; only when there is stillness in movement does the universal rhythm manifest." The actualization of this modern day koan is more accessible than you might think.

Transcending the Line That Doesn't Really Exist

> There is a point where in the mystery of existence contradictions meet; where movement is not all movement and stillness is not all stillness; where the idea and the form, the within and the without, are united; where infinite becomes finite, yet not.
>
> ~ RABINDRANATH TAGORE

Developing the skillfulness to "do" less and "be still" is a high calling and one that is practiced over a lifetime. It invites us to slow down our minds and bodies as we busily scurry around on the horizontal surface of life like frenzied ants; to purposefully pause and descend vertically to our center, wherein we access the true Self that in perfect stillness, patiently awaits our arrival. Eckhart Tolle echoed these sentiments in his poetic book, *Stillness Speaks,* when he wrote, "Your innermost sense of self, of who you are, is inseparable from stillness. This is the I Am that is deeper than name or form." Suffice it to say, Tolle, Holmes, Lee, and many other master teachers believe that stillness creates the sacred opening through which we can fully enter into an experience of our oneness with Life. Once in the portal, the practice is to mindfully plumb the depths and dissolve the misperception that there is a place where the human part of us ends and the sacred Self begins. While it may sound dualistic that we would have to "go" somewhere to enter into God's presence, it really is not, because that intersection is seamless—so much so it doesn't really even exist. Over many millennia religiosity fabricated the intersection in order to externalize God and help sustain a belief in separation from Source. We can transcend and easily disprove this belief in separation, but *only through our own direct experience* with the One. Stillness creates the space to do so... and thus the saying, "Be still and know I Am God."

In Sacred Stillness You'll Connect with Your Authentic Power

> What we are looking for we are looking with.
>
> ~ ERNEST HOLMES

It is in sacred stillness that we discover that this paradoxical quote by Ernest Holmes is quite profound—one with which a true mystic would agree. Consider what a miracle it is that you can observe your mind thinking about the miracle of your life. You can think a thought and at the same time, observe the thought you are thinking about, which means the observer of the thought must be bigger than the thinker of the thought. Imagine just for one moment the power and liberation that comes with the awareness that the true you is far greater than the condition or experience that your thinking mind has you convinced lies before you. Again, stillness is the access point to the "I Am." Stillness awaits you in peaceful silent repose, in the quiet space below the busy-minded thinker that drones on and on about what is happening "out there" on the horizontal plane of life.

> We all have within us a center of stillness surrounded by silence.
>
> ~ DAG HAMMARSKJÖLD

Although stillness and silence are often thought of as the same thing they are really quite different. This is an important distinction to embrace because we need both; they actually work hand-in-hand when it comes to entering the passageway that leads to knowing God's presence in a personal way. In my book *Your (Re)Defining Moments: Becoming Who You Were Born to Be,* the case for this point is made:

While silence opens you to experiencing the absence of noise, stillness is a state of mind you bring into your daily life. Silence and stillness work in tandem, taking us deeper into the realm of the true Self. Silence opens us to experiencing the absence of noise, but stillness sets the stage. It is how the energy of silence is experienced in real time. Finding the richness of deep silence and stillness in our meditation or quiet time at home or in a church sanctuary is an important and beautiful experience. However, when we leave that sacred space, although we may have to leave some portion of our silence behind, too often we also leave our stillness behind. We don't have to do that. Although it seems we may not be able to take total silence with us into our daily lives, we can take stillness along because it is a state of mind and, therefore, not subject to outer conditions unless we allow it to be so. By mindfully taking stillness with us into our daily activities, we are also bringing with us a "portable portal" to inner silence. With a conscious embodiment of stillness, we could be riding Space Mountain at Disneyland and still have access to silence despite the external noise all around us.

The Practice of Becoming an Everyday Mystic

Taking stillness with us into our daily lives may seem a bit overwhelming without some support along the way. Consider the following mindfulness practice as a good place to begin. Remember, mindful breathing is a practice that will help anchor yourself in the moment by slowing down your mind and aligning you with that state of stillness that already exists at your center. In those moments when you may be feeling trapped on the treadmill of "do, do, do" stop and take five long, purposeful, slow and deep breaths, and repeat the process for several minutes.

On the first in-breath silently affirm
Be still and know God is and therefore I am.

On the second in-breath silently affirm
Be still and know God.

On the third in-breath silently affirm
Be still and know.

On the fourth in-breath silently affirm
Be still.

On the fifth in-breath affirm
Be . . . Be . . . Be . . .

The process is like peeling an onion: with each following breath comes a deeper calm, and with calm comes stillness, and with stillness comes inner silence and the opportunity to fully merge with the sacred presence of the One. Something very subtle happens when you breathe mindfully; stillness burbles up from within and fills in the cracks and crevices between your breaths, and you find yourself experiencing your oneness with Life and the peace that passes all understanding. Just imagine, you are only five mindful breaths away from becoming an *everyday* mystic.

HOW AMAZING IS THAT!

There is great power to be found in doing the thing you don't want to do. The question is, How do you do it—where do you start—and when?

Just **Do It!**

> Do something every day that you don't want to do. This is the golden rule for acquiring the habit of doing your duty without pain . . . Duties are not performed for duty's sake, but because their neglect would make the man uncomfortable. A man performs but one duty—the duty of contenting his spirit, the duty of making himself agreeable to himself.
>
> ~ MARK TWAIN

Having just returned from seven wonderful but busy days on the road and feeling very good about what I accomplished, here I sit at my computer and, to be totally transparent with you, the last thing I want to do now is another "thing." My logical mind wanders into a discussion with itself saying, "You've worked hard for the past week and you deserve a break." Clearly, my mind is lobbying for a day with no obligations or commitments whatsoever, but at the same time, it is also aware of the trap it is setting for itself. This is when I become most aware of that place within me wherein instant gratification lies in wait, impatiently chomping at the bit, hoping to ambush and undermine my commitment to my predetermined duties of the day. Then the words of Ralph Waldo Emerson come roaring through my mind like a nonstop train, “Do the thing and you will have the power,” and any semblance of instant gratification is gone, leaving me with no choice; the full-court press is on. I vehemently and swiftly recoil from Emerson’s admonition because it challenges me to live up to my highest potential when I’m really not in the mood for living up to anything.

So goes the journey of a soul wishing to honor its goals, purpose, and evolutionary path; many are those micromoments when the inspiration to do what Emerson refers to as “the thing” we do not want to do comes and goes in a heartbeat. The practice is to initiate *and stay with the action* even after the inspiration has long faded in the wind. This is indeed a high call to duty—to ourselves.

I interpret Twain’s words “doing your duty” as being synonymous with the commitment to one’s self to continually evolve and grow more fully into a being of infinite possibilities by not settling for the road more traveled, which is, without question, the road of instant gratification. In practical application how does the wisdom of Twain and Emerson resonate with you? What does “doing something you don’t want to do” really mean? Does jumping out of an airplane or bungee-jumping off a bridge 300 feet high qualify simply because you are afraid to do so? It could, but it might also include the more mundane, everyday things we often might tend to dodge such as taking out trash, mowing the lawn, doing the dishes, going to the gym, studying for the inevitable test at school, communicating with someone we have been avoiding, finishing that project for work, and so on. Regardless of what it might be, it means putting wheels under that which is ours to do to create a life truly worth living.

Sometimes I have difficulty doing that one extra thing (whatever it may be) even when I know that, as a result, I will have the power Emerson promises. Of course, that power always comes in the form of delayed gratification. There is nothing quite as empowering as the feeling that arises when we stand toe-to-toe with our own dragons of lethargy and slay them. Does this mean we should never take a day off to do absolutely nothing but relax and regenerate? Of course not, but it does mean that when we do take those days, it is sponsored by a conscious proactive choice that is made from a place of authentic power rather than instant gratification or lethargy.

What "duty" might you perform today that would make you, as Twain says, agreeable with yourself? Just choose one thing that is not on the agenda but needs doing, and do it. Once you initiate the action you'll be amazed at how the Universe conspires to do Its part. There is more power available to you than you can possibly imagine when you just do the thing.

YES, NOW.

A life without meaning is joyless
and a life without joy
is meaningless.

Joy Is an Inside Job!

Life is not just something to be endured.
It is to be lived in joy, in a fullness without limit.

~ ERNEST HOLMES, *DISCOVER A RICHER LIFE*

Have you ever given thought to why we experience joy and where that emotion comes from? Joy is the sacred GPS signal your soul transmits when trying to guide you to your bliss, purpose, and, ultimately, the fulfillment of a life worth living. Too many people falsely believe that we can't experience a joy-full life *while* at the same time diligently "working" to create a more productive life—that the two experiences are mutually exclusive—that one must precede the other. Perhaps this belief draws its life from the proverbial Puritan work ethic that in essence, keeps joy shrouded in shame because it's meant to be experienced only in the heavenly Hereafter as a reward for "enduring" life in a human skin.

This underlying belief may be ensconced more deeply in the collective unconscious mind of humankind than we realize, and therefore, it lurks unnoticed in the dark corners of our individual minds. However, with awareness we'll come to see that, as Dr. Holmes suggests, we were not sent here just to endure; we came hardwired to be vessels through which joy flows with grace and ease. Joy is an exquisite part of the package that came with the gift of life and, therefore, it is our divine right—we just have to name it and claim it—and that is our call to action. Embracing the idea that our lives *should be* about more than simply enduring until we exit the planet is a worthy concept to embrace and it begins with a willingness to deeply examine our thoughts and beliefs about life. So, let us begin!

> The artesian well of joy never runs dry.
> We clog it with our thoughts.
>
> ~ DON BLANDING, *JOY IS AN INSIDE JOB*

As a spiritual mentor one of my primary jobs is to guide my clients toward what brings them a sense of fulfillment—a life of purpose and meaning. I point out that one of the telltale signs that we are living our lives "on purpose" is the presence of joy in the doing of whatever is ours to do. What I have learned is that when we are doing that which we were born to do and being who we were born to be, authentic joy seems to show up naturally as part of our experience in the present moment. When this happens our life takes on a hue, depth, and richness that reveal themselves in everything we say and do. The practice is to mindfully become the conscious observer of how, when, and where joy arises in our daily lives—*and* if it doesn't, inquire why. Given the fact that not everyone's life may seem like a joyful experience on a daily basis, with mindfulness it is still possible to put "whatever is" in the current moment on pause long enough to reframe it and, thereby make space for joy to reveal itself in spite of current conditions.

The important thing to remember is that with emotional awareness we will be able to discern those moments when the true Self is trying to get our attention. Naturally, this raises some interesting questions: Where does joy live and how do we know when we are experiencing authentic joy? What is it that opens us to the experience commonly known as joy and is it the same experience for everyone? Is joy more readily available at certain times of the year (such as during the holidays), or is it we who tend to be more available to joy some times more than others? Is the source of our joy internal or external and how can we have more joy in every blessed day? These are all questions that, when examined and understood, will align us with regularly experienced joy, not just as a possibility after our goals and objectives have been met, but as a daily principle as certain and consistent as gravity.

Begin by Discerning the Difference Between Joy and Happiness

The line between joy and happiness can be a gray one but nonetheless, important to discern. Simply put, one is cause and the other is effect. Spiritually speaking, happiness is a derivative of joy, that which we feel welling up from within the core of our being when we are completely aligned with, plugged into, turned on to, and tuned into Life. Happiness that arises *from* joy can happen anytime, anywhere. Next to love, joy is the essence of the Divine in Its highest vibration as it moves through us. Happiness can be thought of as the outer expression of joy —the horn by means of which authentic joy trumpets Spirit's presence in the human condition.

In her brilliant daily blog, *Living Consciously,* my friend and colleague Dr. Carol Carnes further elucidated this idea when she wrote, "Joy is a big word, much bigger than happiness. Joy is a deep response to Being. It is the delight of the soul to be in form and to have experiences that are unavailable in the formless state. How long has it been since you felt its presence in your body, your heart, your mind? Joy takes us out of longing into reality. It is the state of mind where nothing has to happen or be added." Perhaps the invitation Dr. Carnes offers is to stop seeking happiness and begin to open to what poet (and student of Ernest Holmes) Don Blanding referred to as the "artesian well" that flows from the joy of Being.

Joy Flows from Connection—But to What?

> From joy springs all creation, By joy it is sustained,
> Toward joy it proceeds, And unto joy it returns.
>
> ~ *THE UPANISHADS*

In the gathering of insights for this topic, I invited my Facebook friends to share their ideas about joy and how and when it shows up in their lives. While their comments were wonderfully diverse there was also a common thread running through most of them that spoke to the single most important component of joy, which is a sense of *personal connection*. A connection to what? They referred to a connection with a universal Presence some called God (some Nature, some Life) and with loved ones as the conduit through which joy flows in and through their lives.

In essence, when one is feeling *personally* connected to life and engaged in the present moment, joy becomes a natural part of the experience. Ask musicians what they are feeling when performing just for the "joy of it." They will say they are feeling connected to something larger than themselves, they are simply instruments and the music is moving *through* them effortlessly. Ask new parents what they are feeling as they cradle their newborn baby—a precious gift from beyond this world of flesh and bone. They will say they are feeling the joy of *oneness* and the miracle of life. Simply put, a connection with life in the present moment primes the pump for joy.

Joy is the infallible sign of the Presence of God.

~ PIERRE TEILHARD DE CHARDIN

In many spiritual traditions Joy is considered another name for Infinite Presence expressing through us in those moments when we most feel our unity with life and one another. In this light we could say that joy is the heart throb of the Infinite, pulsating in and through each of us in those moments when we feel a sense of connection to what matters and what is real. Most often this will center on our relationships. Whether it is a relationship we are having with our loved ones, including the dog (or cat), strangers, nature's creatures, or the planet itself, what matters most, and what brings the most joy, are relationships where there is a feeling of personal connection. Perhaps that's because in those moments of feeling connected to the people and things that matter, we are also (knowingly or unknowingly) experiencing the deepest connection—the greatest relationship of all—which is our unity with the Universe itself. Irrespective of where we are or what we are doing—whether we are working diligently to create a life worth living or playing hard to celebrate a life worth living—joy brings with it a sense of wholeness where all sense of separation dissolves.

Moving Into Our House of Joy

> If you knew yourself for even one moment,
> if you could just glimpse your most beautiful
> face, maybe you wouldn't slumber so deeply
> in that house of clay. Why not move into your
> house of joy and shine into every crevice!
> For you are the secret Treasure-bearer, and
> always have been. Didn't you know?
>
> ~ RUMI

The "house of clay" Rumi speaks of is that aspect of our being that so easily gets seduced by, and caught up in, the gravitational pull of the human condition—it is the physical and emotional part of us that looks outward to the world for our sense of wholeness, happiness and joy. Conversely, to move into our "house of joy" means taking the vertical plunge inward, from our head to our heart, where the ineffable presence of the One is so strongly felt, embodied, and then actualized in our daily lives. Ultimately, joy truly is an inside job; it has taken up residence in our minds and hearts and, therefore, is *always* on call, waiting to be activated and integrated in our lives and the lives of others. We cannot give others our joy because we cannot give them that which they already have—however, we can be the stimulus that invokes joy to arise from *within themselves.* Joy is a subtle energy; it is as intangible as the air we breathe, and yet as palpable as our heartbeat—as difficult to describe as is love, and yet as easy to feel as love itself.

As previously mentioned, many people embody the false notion that we can't experience a joy-full life while at the same time diligently "working" to create a more productive life. The practice is to know that one complements the other and to find balance between the two. As you move through this day may you remember that you don't need a special dispensation to be joy-full . . . you don't have to wait for special occasions to be the beneficiary of authentic joy because there is never a moment when joy is further away than your next thought—lo, your very next breath. Joy is the artesian well that can never run dry because its source is Infinite. The practice is to turn within and embrace a high thought—one that connects you with who you truly are and to what really matters—while deeply feeling your unity with all of Life in the present moment. Trust it is the calling of your heart to naturally wrap itself around that image, and know that joy will ascend surely as does the morning sun. It must, because you have primed the pump of the artesian well within.

May you know the depths of a joy so rich and meaningful that you can't help but share it with your world this day and every day.

YOU MATTER.

Living in the fast lane of life is a much more enjoyable experience if you can practice mindfulness along the way.

Honk If You Love **Harmony on the Highway!**

Have you ever noticed that anybody driving slower than you is an idiot, and anyone going faster than you is a maniac?

~ GEORGE CARLIN

George Carlin makes a good point when he implies that anyone driving other than how we do has got it wrong. Clearly he is poking fun at us but have you ever thought of your car as a mobile learning laboratory and the roads upon which you drive as places where great discoveries about yourself and others can be made? If we are fully conscious, these discoveries often have less to do with how we are driving and more about the fact that sometimes our conscious mind is someplace other than in our body which is piloting tons of metal down a concrete launching strip often at an accelerated rate of speed. The point is, we have to be mindfully conscious and present in the moment to catch ourselves in the act and opportunities to do so are abundant, especially if we have a cell phone and drive a car.

In California the use of a cell phone (as a "handheld" device) while driving is illegal, and yet it is not at all uncommon to see a person zooming down the highway, cruising through an intersection, or sitting at a stoplight either texting or talking on his cellphone. I believe we have become addicted to mobile devices; they offer a form of instant gratification that creates an immediate diversion from being fully present in the moment. The diversions that keep us separated from the present moment are legion and the mobile device is but one of them. I find this to be a curious thing given the fact that most of us know that anytime our focus of attention is divided we are less effective at everything we are doing and driving is certainly no exception to the rule. Although multitasking may be considered a great skill there are times when it can also be a less than productive endeavor if it severs our thinking mind from what our body is doing in any given moment.

While this may seem like a diatribe regarding our driving skills (please notice I include myself in this category), I hope you'll see that it is far more than that. It really is a reminder about practicing mindfulness everywhere in our lives—it's about developing the skillfulness to be 100 percent present in the moment with whatever we are doing. The same mindfulness practice can be applied to how, when, and where we eat our meals, or how present and engaged we are in our relationships with people when we communicate with them, and so on. Because most of us can relate, I offer the example of using cell phones while we drive only as a method of hooking your attention to examine the larger issue: Having our conscious mind present and accounted for in our body is a wise practice regardless of where our body is or what it may be doing. We'll always be better off for it and so will all of those around us.

When we are mindfully present in the moment energy seems to flow with a greater sense of harmony, grace, and ease, which ultimately manifests as a sense of inner peace. If harmony, grace, ease, and inner peace appeal to you, I invite you to join me in the following mindfulness practice:

As challenging as it may be, the next time you get in your car turn off your mobile devices and put them in your glove box, pocket, purse, briefcase, or any place where you will not be tempted to use them. This applies even if you have a hands-free device, and this includes any type of headphones—we're talking total disconnection from anything but driving the car. This is not just about being present with the experience of consciously piloting your car; in truth it's about being present with yourself—your car just happens to be one of those places one seldom thinks of practicing the Presence. Are you already feeling the separation anxiety?

- Make a commitment to yourself not to use your mobile device until after you have stopped and parked the car.

- While driving, take note of how seductive the wandering mind can be. If the urge arises to reach for your device, take a deep breath and bring your full attention back into your body . . . imagine yourself as being one with the automobile knowing it requires your total integrated attention to function properly and safely.

- When you park your car and shut off the engine, just sit for a moment—before you reach for your devices—and breathe. Then notice how much more present you are and how much more peaceful you feel.

The happy result of this mindfulness practice is that not only is the road a more pleasant and safe place to be, but you'll get an opportunity to share some quality one-on-one time with the person with whom you probably spend the least amount of time—yourself—and that's always a beautiful thing.

HONK IF YOU LOVE HARMONY, GRACE, EASE, AND INNER PEACE ON THE HIGHWAY OF LIFE!

The Law of Attraction guarantees that complainers will always have a lifetime supply of things to complain about.

The **Complaint Department** Is Closed!

> You could write a song about some kind of emotional problem you are having, but it would not be a good song, in my eyes, until it went through a period of sensitivity to a moment of clarity. Without that moment of clarity to contribute to the song, it's just complaining.
>
> ~ JONI MITCHELL

Do you know any chronic complainers? They focus on some situation, person, condition, or problem they don't like and it becomes their story. They tell it over and over again to anyone who will listen and, hopefully, commiserate with them. The danger in being a chronic complainer is that the universe is listening; it takes what we focus our energy on and expands our experience of it. In other words, the more we complain about something, the more we will draw to ourselves things to complain about.

If you ever find yourself complaining about something, you'll notice that you are most likely feeling a sense of agitation which then leads to emotional suffering. A fast track to inner peace is to be mindful enough when you are complaining to pause for a moment of clarity. The practice is to put what you are complaining about into one of two categories. Either it's an issue you can do something about, and if so, you have an opportunity to change it; or it's beyond your control, in which case your only alternative is to change your perspective and accept that it is what it is, which, in turn, can change your experience. Doing neither means you can continue to suffer.

As an example, on a recent trip to Italy with my wife, I caught myself complaining about how unbearably hot it was, which was exacerbated by the massive number of people jamming themselves into the same space I was. I became aware of how much I was complaining only when I heard myself commiserating with complete strangers who didn't even speak the same language as I! I was focusing so much on my misery that I seemed to magnetically attract only those people who would support me in my suffering. Funny how the law of attraction works, isn't it?

Then in a moment of clarity I got it. The unbearable heat and the countless number of people everywhere were two things I had absolutely no control over and focusing on them only made it worse. As always, it came down to the fact that I was at choice. I could push against the prevailing heat wave and hoards of people and in the process, become increasingly more miserable, or I could choose to change my perspective and see it all through new eyes, which is exactly what I did. I began to focus on how amazingly blessed and fortunate I was to be able to travel abroad under any conditions. Beyond that, I also chose to cease commiserating with anyone who wanted to talk about how miserable the heat was. All I can say is, that one small shift in perspective changed my experience for the balance of the trip.

We don't have to travel in the month of August to find something or someone to complain about—we can find it right here at home! We need look no further than the morning newspaper or the six-o'clock news—it seems "Breaking News" is always happening. If we are susceptible to commiserating with others about how bad or wrong someone or something is the negative vortex will suck us right in. At times it seems as if complainers have us surrounded, which is why remembering that we can make conscious choices is so important—we can choose to be one of them or we can choose to mindfully transcend the gravitational pull of their energy.

The Practice Is to Seek a Moment of Clarity

> What you're supposed to do when you don't like a thing is change it. If you can't change it, change the way you think about it. Don't complain.
>
> ~ MAYA ANGELOU

When we pause for a moment of conscious clarity around that which we are complaining about, it naturally provides the possibility to redirect the energy in a more productive way. Irrespective of the issue, the practice is to be mindful that, with clarity, we can remember to put whatever we are tempted to complain about into one of the two categories I mentioned earlier: either it's an issue we can do something about, or it's beyond our control. The choice is always ours. As a rule of thumb, constant complainers are not doers—they are watchers hoping someone else will be motivated enough by their complaining to do something on their behalf. Perhaps the best call to action is to remember that whenever we complain we are simply granting that which we are complaining about permission to remain unchanged in our experience.

As Joni Mitchell says, the song (your story) you are singing may need a moment of clarity. So the next time you catch yourself complaining about anything, pause, breathe, and seek a moment of clarity about the issue at hand and in the process you just may choose to change your tune. At the end of the day you'll be a much happier camper and so will those around you.

AND THAT'S A GOOD THING.

Be sure you put your feet in the right place,
then stand firm.

~ ABRAHAM LINCOLN

Before You Can Stand in Your Power You Have to Know Where to **Look for It**

> It has taken humanity thousands of years to learn that it has the power to control its own destiny . . . we must realize that we are using a Power, compared to which the united intelligence of the human race is as nothing.
>
> ~ ERNEST HOLMES

People all over the planet want it. Many work hard for it. Legions go to war for it. Others steal or lie for it. Some envy those whom they perceive as having more of it than they. In short, a majority of people on the planet believe there is a dire shortage of it and they'll do just about anything to get more of it. What is "it"? POWER. It is the one thing that we as human beings tend to live in fear of not having, and it is this belief that sponsors most human conflict and struggle. This fear divides families, cultures, religions, political parties, and countries. The irony is, there is no shortage of power and never has been; this is a human-made myth that has been perpetuated globally for millennia, and therefore, only humans can rectify the problem. However, before we can logically arrive at that conclusion—and how to transcend that belief—let us explore where this misbelief about a power shortage draws its supposed life force.

We are *all* interested in power in one form or another and most of us desire to have more of it because, somehow, we have bought into the idea that when we have enough power, then and only then, will we feel safe enough, respected enough, important enough, needed enough, secure enough, and perhaps, at peace enough. In other words there is a plethora of "not enoughness" at the core of powerlessness. I have to admit that for my first twenty-eight years on the planet, power was something I believed I was sorely lacking and it played out in numerous ways. Then one night in my first Science of Mind class, my teacher, William Curtiss, introduced me to Dr. Ernest Holmes when he played a tape recording of Holmes's classic radio program, *This Thing Called Life*. That was the moment my understanding of power and how I had been looking for it in all the wrong places deepened. The first words Holmes spoke were, "There is a Power for good in the Universe, greater than you are, and you can use It." Suffice it to say, he had me at hello. The lingering question for this novitiate was, where is it and how soon can I get some? I would soon have that answer and in the process discover what standing in *my* power really meant . . . and it would change my life forever.

How You Define Power Determines Where You Will Seek It

Perhaps the problem originates with the fact that power means different things to different people, and therefore, the source of one's power can appear to have different points of origination. To determine our personal definition of power, the quintessential question is where do we look for it. This is a query humankind has wrestled with from antiquity and it is worthy of investigation because the answer will shape not only the life that we have come here to live, but the world in which we live. When you think of the word "power" what image comes to mind? That image is probably different from what your neighbor might have in mind, or the individual driving in the lane next to you on the freeway, or a person on the other side of the planet . . . but make no mistake about it, they *do* have a belief about what power is and where it comes from. For the environmentalist, power may be something that comes through solar panels directly from the sun. For a cabinetmaker, power may be what he gets when he connects his radial saw to an electrical wall outlet. For a politician, power might come by garnering more votes than her opponent. For the codependent, power might come from controlling other people's behavior. For some, power may be gained by getting another person's approval or love. For the addict, power may come by means of his substance of choice. For a Wall Street banker, power might be determined by who has the most money in the coffers at the end of the day, while for a battlefield general it may mean having the biggest arsenal. For the one praying for divine intervention, power may be sought from a sky God somewhere in the heavens above.

> Authentic power is the real deal.
> You can't inherit it, buy it, or win it.
> You also can't lose it.
> You don't need to build your body,
> reputation, wealth, or charisma to get it.
>
> ~ GARY ZUKAV

The only drawback with looking to any of the aforementioned sources for our power is that they are external and therefore subject to what lies outside of us rather than what lies within. In his groundbreaking book, *The Seat of the Soul,* Gary Zukav affirms that we are all on a quest for power; the question is, where are we looking for that power? If we turn within, toward the authentic Self, what we'll find there is what he coined "authentic power"; if we turn outward to the world, our quest leads us to pursue what he called "external power." The primary difference between authentic power and external power is that one is internally and eternally available to us while the other is always temporal, subject to coming and going, depending on outer current conditions which can at times leave us feeling powerless. When we feel powerless, the tendency is to seek power in external things such as money, position, physical strength, beauty, sexuality, possessions, job titles, and so on—all of which fuel the egoic self's ongoing quest for even more external power because it knows it has no power of its own. The ego draws 100 percent of its identity, power, and life-force from the world. If we are not mindful, it is quite easy to allow these external things to define us. At the end of the day, if we are reliant on these forms of external power, we'll have no alternative but to feel vulnerable, powerless and uncertain of who we really are.

The majority of people pursue external power because it appears in such seductive, tangible, and accessible ways that can be "objectified, measured, and compared" with other people's "power." The endgame is "power struggles" that result in a "mine is bigger/better than yours—and thus I am more powerful than you" mindset. The only source of power that is unmeasurable, incomparable, inexhaustible, changeless, consistent, and equally available to all without struggle is that which Masters throughout the ages have referred to as the Original Self, known by many names including God. It is that place within us wherein absolute Power is making Itself available to us every moment of every day. Ernest Holmes summarized this idea in a truly elegant way in his book *Creative Mind:*

> We have within us a power that is greater than anything that we shall ever contact in the outer, a power that can overcome every obstacle in our life and set us safe, satisfied and at peace, healed and prosperous, in a new light, and in a new life. Mind, all mind, is right here. It is God's Mind, God's creative Power, God's creative Life. We have as much of this Power to use in our daily life as we can believe in and embody.

The Question Is, How Much Power Can You Embody?

The operative word is "embody," which can be thought of as personifying or personalizing an idea by means of our feeling nature—to have a full realization in our emotional and physical body of that which our mind already knows is innately true. To fully embody God's presence and power is to *feel* It coursing through every fiber of our being, spiritually, emotionally, mentally, and physically. When this happens, every muscle, sinew, organ, nerve, and bone of our being experiences a quickened vibration and something exquisitely subtle arises from within. We begin to see what lies "out there" differently—our perception of ourselves and the world shifts because we intuitively *know* there has been a power shift within. As a result, we stand more erect, speak with more clarity and confidence, make wiser choices, and perhaps, most importantly, we live with transparency, passion, authentic joy, and reverence, knowing we walk a sacred earth. When we fully embody God's presence at the center and circumference of our being we will then comprehend the true essence of "Standing in our Power." This is the moment we are literally set free from the tyranny of external power because we have awakened; we have become fully conscious and one with the source of our authentic power that comes from the deep reservoir of Infinite Presence within. Standing in our power is *always* an inside job.

The Transformative Moment Happens When We Move From WANTING Power to BEING Power

I offer this simple five-step Mindfulness Practice as a place to begin standing in your own power:

1. **Remember the presence** of God is always where you are: have faith that the Infinite Intelligence that put you here is closer to you than your very breath.
2. **Focus your mind** on the moment, which is your only point of power.
3. **Invoke the awareness** of God's presence at the center of your being through continued, conscious, intentional breathing: on your in-breath affirm, "God is" and on your out-breath

affirm, "I am." This is where wanting power transforms into being power.

4. **Embody the fact** that you have just entered a partnership with an expanding Universe that is Omnipotent. Experience the limitless Power that animates all life, creates galaxies, holds the stars in place, causes the tides to ebb and flow, and makes all things possible surging through you at the core of your being.
5. **Invite this Infinite Power** to guide you in your words, deeds, and actions, knowing that, not only are you using It, It is using you as a force for good in your life and the world.

To stand in your authentic power is to give yourself permission to live life fully engaged, while transcending the need to enter into the power struggles that the world says are necessary to create a life of wholeness, purpose, and meaning. It is then that you shall fully understand what Holmes meant when he said there is a power for good in the universe and you can use it. Where you look for your power will determine the amount of it you can access. May Abraham Lincoln's words, "Be sure you put your feet in the right place, then stand firm," be forever etched on the walls of your heart and mind. Standing *in* your power is the mindfulness practice of remembering that the "right place" is always right where you are in *every* sacred moment.

AND IT'S ONLY ONE BREATH AWAY.

Having a vision for your life is wise counsel;
it serves as a compass that guides your mind to your
ultimate destination—a life worth living.

Stand in Your Vision and **Look Up!**

A rock pile ceases to be a rock pile the moment a man contemplates it, bearing within him the image of a Cathedral.

~ ANTOINE DE SAINT-EXUPÉRY

Several years ago while in Barcelona, Spain, I had the opportunity to visit Catalan architect Antoni Gaudi's Sagrada Família. Although not officially a cathedral because it is not yet the seat of a bishop, it is often thought of as such because it stands as tall or taller than many ancient cathedrals. What is unique about the structure is that, while Gothic in design, it is also very Art Nouveau and unlike any other cathedral ever built; it is one of a kind, in a class of its own. If you have ever seen pictures of it you'll understand why I call it one of a kind. I encourage you to Google "Sagrada Família" and see for yourself—it is quite unusual and magnificent.

Gaudi designed and took over construction of the project in 1883, and to this day, it is still a work in progress. It stands taller than many skyscrapers; scaffolding and huge mechanical cranes loom on the skyline. The completion of the project is tentatively set for 2026, the centennial of Gaudi's passing. It is said that he devoted the best of his years to the project, and at the time of his passing at age 73 in 1926, less than a quarter of it was complete.

One-hundred and twenty-eight years after his vision was cast, I humbly stood at the base of this monolithic structure and gazed skyward wondering how much more had to be done to complete his vision. My mind raced back to the year 1883 when there was little more than barren land and rocks in that spot and I imagined him standing there, looking up, seeing his masterpiece in its completed form. That's what visionaries do—they see their dream in its completed form long before it is realized in the material world. The transformation of concrete and rocks into a cathedral happened long before Gaudi's workers ever broke ground...and the fact that they are still working on the manifestation of it proves it was a very big vision.

Do you have a vision for your Life, and if so, how big is it?

If you have a vision for your life, can you see yourself living that life *now,* even if the outer manifestation of it isn't yet visible? If not, perhaps your vision isn't big enough. While many say you have to see it to believe it, others are saying that you have to believe it to see it. Which are you? This is where and when the foundation for a life worth living is established. The practice is to contemplate your life's greatest dream as Gaudi contemplated his cathedral—as a completed idea in the creative Mind of a Universe that knows no limitations. In other words, the sky really is the limit; the only caveat is that this creative

Mind is waiting for you to upload the design blueprints known as your belief system. What is your vision for your life? Are you looking up, or looking down? Be mindful of where your predominate thoughts go, because whether you are aware of it or not, that is the design plan you are uploading.

If you believe enough in your vision it will take on a life of its own.

Clearly, Gaudi believed in his vision, so much so that it had no alternative but to become a reality, even years after his passing. A clear, fully embodied vision is a powerful tool because it takes on a life of its own. In other words, turning a pile of rocks into a cathedral isn't difficult once you have faithfully surrendered to the vision—the Universe conspires to support you in your vision if you are willing to stand in it, own it, and take the necessary actions to move it forward. A vision isn't created by just wishing it will happen.

We are all visionaries—that is to say, we each hold in our mind a vision for our life: what it can or can't be, might or might not be, or will or won't be. So the question really isn't, do you have a vision for your life—if you are alive you have a vision. The real question is, *what* is your vision? Are you looking down at the rocks or up to the sky? Remember, the Universe is listening.

AND IT'S ALREADY UPLOADING YOUR BLUEPRINTS.

Are you putting your life on hold
and waiting for the "right time" to enjoy it?

The Ride of Your Life Doesn't Start Somewhere Down the Road

> Life should not be a journey to the grave with the intention of arriving safely in a pretty and well preserved body, but rather to skid in broadside in a cloud of smoke, thoroughly used up, totally worn out, and loudly proclaiming, "Wow! What a Ride!"
>
> ~ HUNTER S. THOMPSON

One of my most vivid memories as a kid growing up in the 1950s pertains to the sofa in the family room of our home. The reason I remember this particular sofa so well is that my mom covered it with a custom-fitted, clear piece of vinyl plastic, just like so many people did in that era. In the summertime I would perspire profusely and whenever I sat on the sofa in shorts and a shirt my skin would stick to the plastic as if it was glued there—it was torture each time I would move or get up from the sofa. My mom's logic was that this was an expensive sofa so she was preserving it for greater longevity and enjoyment somewhere down the road and for years to come. Longevity maybe—enjoyment . . . umm, not so much. I don't know where that sofa eventually ended up but I am quite sure some of my hide is still firmly adhered to it.

That sofa experience serves as a perfect metaphor for how many of us live our lives. Perhaps it's just human nature to put off fully enjoying the moment and whatever it entails until we arrive at that etheric place called "somewhere down the road" where and when the time will be more appropriate to enjoy the experience. I am not talking about spending money we don't have or doing perilous and unintelligent things with our possessions and/or our bodies. I am talking about living in the richness that each day offers in a manner that allows us to experience the blessing of being alive today rather than postponing it until further notice somewhere down the road. The reality check for me is this: the older I grow, the more I know this moment is as good as it gets because it's the only moment I have. So why not live in it as deeply and richly as I can? While this topic is not just about the wisdom with which we use our financial resources, I've known more than one person who postponed enjoying the fruits of his labor, squirreling away every penny he earned, saving it for a rainy day. This is not an indictment of saving wisely—it's an indictment of saving fearfully in a manner that robs us of what joy the moment might bring if we only allow ourselves to be open to it.

Recently, I saw a 40-foot motorhome with a fancy boat in tow being driven down the freeway. A bumper sticker on it said, "We're spending our kids' inheritance NOW and enjoying every dime of it!" As I drove by I noticed that the driver was not an elderly man who had "paid his dues" (which I expected to see), but a much younger man than me. I thought to myself, why not—you have earned it; if you can afford it, you should enjoy it while you have the opportunity to. At first this mindset can appear self-serving and perhaps a bit stingy, but taken in proper context, it is not that at all; it's about being wise enough to know what you are worthy of and embracing it while you can. For some it may be about no longer postponing the motor-home experience or taking the trip of a lifetime until "someday" arrives. For others it may be about no longer postponing joining that hiking club, planting that garden, or enrolling in that long desired art, dance, fitness, or computer class until such time when it is more convenient or practical. Seldom does that time ever show up.

From a spiritual perspective, we know that life is eternal —and that is a profoundly important thing to remember. However, equally important we know we exist on a timeline— our life has an expiration date. It's a gift meant to be fully used before we leave the planet rather than squandered by living small. In short, don't return to your Maker less than fully "used up." That's like paying for a full day pass at Disneyland and then leaving the park before you get to all the rides. You have already paid the admission price for the ride called life, so be sure to get your money's worth before you leave.

What might you be postponing until that etheric destination called "somewhere down the road"? Perhaps now is the time to stop thinking and start doing. Of course, that will always be the case because now is all there is and now is all you have. How are you spending your "now"?

AT THE END OF YOUR
JOURNEY ON THIS PLANET, WHENEVER
THAT DAY COMES, MAY YOU
BE ABLE TO SAY,
"WOW! WHAT A RIDE!"

Why struggle to open a door between us when the whole wall is an illusion?

~ RUMI

One Vine — Many Branches

SPIRIT IS ALL—the Center and Circumference of everything that exists—both manifest and unmanifest. It has no enemies, no differences, no otherness, no apartness, no separation from Itself. It is Undivided, Complete and Perfect within Itself, having no opposites and no opposition.

~ ERNEST HOLMES, *THE SCIENCE OF MIND*

Try this experiment with me. Before reading the second paragraph, I invite you to pause at the end of this paragraph for just sixty seconds and ponder this question: Why are you reading this book—what is it that has compelled you to invest your precious time and resources to explore *Encouraging Words*?

Although the thoughts and words that float to the top of your awareness may be different from mine, I propose that the *feelings* that wrap themselves around those thoughts and words are probably the same. Reading spiritually uplifting ideas helps us intuit a sense of hope, faith, courage, and perhaps most significantly, a feeling of connectedness and oneness with something larger than ourselves. This feeling, in turn, sublimates as the ineffable energy we know as inner peace, which is what every human being longs for. Ultimately, the sense of connection and oneness we feel subtly arises from our embodied belief that, as Ernest Holmes so eloquently summarized, Spirit is all there is—period. Speaking spiritually and metaphorically, there is One Vine and many branches, so perhaps the koan (or divine paradox) is "Where on the Vine of Life do I end and you begin?" Holmes's statement is so profound because it leaves no wiggle room for "yeah-buts" or exemptions from the Truth on those special occasions when we might be inclined to believe otherwise. We are One . . . and the impact of this truth is far reaching —*very far reaching.*

What we do to one, we do to all.
What we do for one, we do for all.

> Humankind has not woven the web of life. We are but one thread within it. Whatever we do to the web, we do to ourselves. All things are bound together. All things connect.
>
> ~ CHIEF SEATTLE

Recently, while strolling with my grandson through a very crowded zoo in Santiago, Chile, I witnessed a wonderful example of our connectedness being played out as a long line of young children paraded past me being led by their teacher. What struck me was that each child was holding the hand of both the child in front and the one in back of him. Clearly this was so none of them wandered off and became separated from the group. Always looking for the perfect metaphors life offers when I am present enough to see them, I was struck by the image before me: Human beings, connected to one another, leading one another, supporting each other, trusting people down the line they can't even see as they journey through the strange and grand adventureland of life. The awareness I had was that something profoundly reassuring comes with the simple realization that we are not alone on the journey—that we are all connected at some level—that the actions of one person can affect another person, which in turn, affects another, and yet another. With this awareness comes the realization that if what we do in life affects others, should not our actions be conducted mindfully *and* purposefully?

TOGETHER WE ARE ONE

A song needs a singer for it to be sung
A bell needs a ringer for it to be rung,
The sky needs the sun to give it light
And the stars need the darkness to shine so bright.

The rain needs the clouds, the clouds need the sky
Birds need the wind to soar and to fly,
The rose needs the rain to help it grow
And the stream needs the ocean for it to flow.

Can you not hear the music play?
Can you not hear the Universe say
That we are all one family, yes we are One.

War needs peace to heal the hate
And fear needs love, and love just can't wait,

> We need each other, oh, can't you see?
> Yes I need you and you need me!
>
> And together, all together, we are One.

Above are some of the lyrics to a song I wrote and recorded in 1982, a few years after discovering the teachings of Science of Mind. While the song was never a commercial hit, the words became deeply etched in the walls of my mind and heart as a mantra, reminding me on countless occasions that we are all connected—that in our oneness we need the unique contrast of one another—and that what affects one affects the many. On the Great Ocean of Life we are each so exquisitely interwoven that we can't help but create ripples and waves that affect others.

What Kind of Ripples and Waves Will You Make?

The takeaway is that you really do matter; everything you do has an impact on someone, somewhere, even if you don't know him or her. Think of yourself as a pebble sending out ripples that grow into waves which continue to touch other lives far beyond your knowing reach. It could be a stranger on the other side of town who is affected by a kind word you extend to your neighbor who, in turn, extends an act of kindness to that person. Then again, it could be a person on the other side of the planet who is affected via the ripple effect initiated by you when you post that special picture or story on Facebook that opens hearts and puts a smile on everyone's face which they then share with others, and so on it goes . . . and the wave grows. So the question we must ask ourselves isn't, "Will we make a difference in the world?" Knowing we are one—and understanding the power of the ripple effect—the real question is, "What kind of difference will it be?" That is how much *you* matter.

As you finish reading this book, may the ripples and waves you send forth from this day and beyond be guided by the impulse of loving-kindness, selflessness, non-judgment, reverence, compassion, and joy. This is what our world needs now and you are the perfect pebble to make some mighty waves. May you live today so fully immersed in the awareness of your oneness with all of Life that any perceived walls separating you from the world dissolve into the nothingness from which they came. Where on the Vine of Life do I end and you begin? Ah! Sweet mystery of Life:

THE ANSWER
IS BURIED IN THE UNFATHOMABLE
PARADOX OF ONENESS . . .

If you love what you make of your life and hold nothing back, life will love you in return.

And in **the End** . . .

It's like, at the end, there's this surprise quiz: am I proud of me? I gave my life to become the person I am right now! Was it worth what I paid?

~ RICHARD BACH

It is said "The End" was the last song the Beatles recorded together as a group—and the last song Lennon and McCartney ever coauthored as a writing team. It is probably one of the shortest songs ever penned but also one of the most profound. The entire lyric is only twenty-eight words, of which the last fifteen are "and in the end the love you take is equal to the love you make."

That's it! What a statement about cause and effect—*and,* what an exquisite way for a creative force known as the Beatles to dissolve into the ethers forever, while at the same time, having that for which they stood continue to reverberate from one generation to the next and to the next. "The End" isn't a love song, it's a song *about* love. A song about understanding that at the end of the day, our lives matter because they are a composition of the minutes, days, and years that we exchange for the privilege of living in a human skin—and love is the medium by which we measure a life worth living.

The "group," the Beatles, technically died at the end of that recording session but their music lives on in you and me. I believe that is because they truly loved what they did and that love found its way into our hearts. They brought the best of themselves together to co-create something none of them could have created alone. However, they also knew when it was time to go their separate ways because their co-creative energy was spent; they knew they were not giving the group, the Beatles, the "best" of themselves any longer.

Because they loved what they created when they were together, they held nothing back, and I think that is the message of this song (and this book). Love what you do; love what you make of your life—hold nothing back—and life will love you in return. I invite you to just sit with this thought for a moment and see where it lands in your mind and heart. This is the question worth pondering as our journey together through *Encouraging Words* comes to completion: In the end, when you leave this planet, will there be a surplus, or a deficit of love left in the wake of your life? Love who you are and love what you do with who you are, and the answer to that question will be self-evident. "All you need is love" isn't just another Beatles' song title—it's the calling of a lifetime.

NEVER FORGET, *YOU* MATTER.

PEACE. DENNIS

About the **Author**

Throughout his lifetime, Dennis Merritt Jones has been on a quest to inspire and lift people to a higher expression of life. His personal vision is to guide people to their purpose, knowing that when we fully awaken to who we are and why we are on the planet, we begin to naturally share our gift with humankind, and in the process, create an enriching life for ourselves and the world around us. Dennis has been a Science of Mind minister since 1985 and received his Doctorate of Divinity in 1996.

Dennis is the author of the award-winning books, *The Art of Uncertainty: How to Live in the Mystery of Life and Love It* and *The Art of Being: 101 Ways to Practice Purpose in Your Life,* as well as *Your (Re)Defining Moments: Becoming Who You Were Born to Be,* all released by Tarcher/Penguin publishing. In addition he is the author of *How to Speak Science of Mind,* published by DeVorss and Company. Look for his latest book, *The Art of Abundance: Ten Rules for a Prosperous Life,* to be released by TarcherPerigee/Penguin Random House Publishing in 2018. Dennis is a columnist for the *Huffington Post* and the *Science of Mind* magazine, as well as various print media. He is also proud to serve as a consultant and spiritual mentor to organizations and individuals in many parts of the world.

Dennis believes we each have the capacity, and ultimately, the responsibility to contribute something positive to this world, leaving it a better place than it was when we arrived —concepts reflected in his writings and seminars. He uses his understanding of universal principles to draw upon wisdom from both Eastern and Western philosophies. Dennis believes that the consciousness of unity, cooperation, and reverence for life on the planet will be one of the most significant influences upon society as we approach the challenges and uncertainties of twenty-first-century living.

Contact Information
Please visit www.DennisMerrittJones.com

Recommended **Reading**

Astin, John. *This Is Always Enough.* United Kingdom: Non-Duality Press, 2007.

———. *Too Intimate for Words.* Santa Cruz: Integrative Arts, 2005.

Chopra, Deepak. *The Seven Spiritual Laws of Success.* New York: Amber-Allen, 1994.

Ferrucci, Piero. *The Power of Kindness.* New York: Tarcher/Penguin, 2006.

Hanh, Thich Nhat. *The Heart of the Buddha's Teaching.* New York: Broadway Books, 1998.

Holmes, Ernest. *Creative Mind.* Cosimo Classics. April 1, 2007.

———. *The Science of Mind.* New York: G. P. Putnam's Sons, 1938.

———. *This Thing Called You.* New York: Tarcher/Penguin, 2004.

Jones, Dennis Merritt. *The Art of Being: 101 Ways to Practice Purpose in Your Life.* New York: Tarcher/Penguin, 2008.

———. *The Art of Uncertainty: How to Live in the Mystery of Life and Love It.* New York: Tarcher/Penguin, 2011.

———. *How to Speak Science of Mind.* Camarillo, CA: DeVorss, 2010.

———. *Your (Re)Defining Moments: Becoming Who You Were Born to Be.* New York: Tarcher/Penguin, 2014.

Science of Mind magazine. Golden, CO: Centers for Spiritual Living.

Zukav, Gary. *The Seat of the Soul.* New York: Fireside, 1989.

Made in the USA
Middletown, DE
02 September 2017